The Saga of Gisli
The Outlaw

TRANSLATED FROM THE ICELANDIC BY

GEORGE JOHNSTON

NOTES AND AN INTRODUCTORY ESSAY BY

PETER FOOTE

UNIVERSITY OF TORONTO PRESS
TORONTO   BUFFALO

© J.M. Dent & Sons Ltd, 1963
First published 1963 in Canada and the United States
by University of Toronto Press
Toronto   Buffalo
Reprinted in paperback 1973, 1978, 1984, 1987, 1992, 1995
ISBN 0 8020 6219 9
Printed in Canada

Canadian Cataloguing in Publication Data

Gîsla saga Súrssonar
The saga of Gisli the outlaw

"The text ... is that ... of Vestfiröinga sögur,
edited by Björn K. Pórólfsson in the series 'Islenzk
Fornrit' (volume vi, Reykjavik, 1943) ... based on
manuscript AM 556a 4to (Arnamagnáèan Institute,
University of Copenhagen)" – p. ix.
"A list of translations of Icelandic texts": p. 90–92.
ISBN 0-8020-6219-9

I. Johnston, George, 1913 Oct. 7–   . II. Foote,
Peter G., 1924–   . III. Title. IV. Title:
Vestfiröinga sögur.

PT7269.G4E5   839.6′3   C74-003207-0

Contents

Acknowledgments

Five people especially have influenced this work for the better: Ian Maxwell of Melbourne, Gabriel Turville-Petre of Oxford, Dag Strömbäck of Uppsala, Björn Þorsteinsson of Reykjavík, and Magnús bóndi Kristjánsson of Botn in Geirþjófsfjörður.

Eiríkur Benedikz of London has kindly read the book in proof.

The Story and the People

THE SAGA OF Gisli was written in Iceland in the early part of the thirteenth century. It is an imaginative reconstruction based on the career of a man and his family who came from Norway to Iceland about A.D. 950 and made their home in Haukadal on the Dyrafjord in the far north-west of the country. The opening chapters tell of the family in Norway and events that led to their voyage to Iceland. The characters and their relationship in this part are most clearly shown by this family tree:

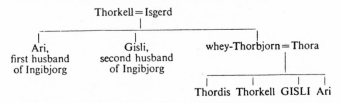

Gisli, son of whey-Thorbjorn, was outlawed for manslaughter in 964, and he then lived in hiding in the north-west of Iceland until his enemies finally caught and killed him in 978. Apart from Gisli and his sister and brothers, the chief characters in this main part of the story are:

Aud, daughter of Vestein, Gisli's wife.

Vestein, son of Vestein, brother of Aud, Gisli's close friend.

      Gunnhild, Vestein's wife.

      Berg | Vestein's sons.
      Helgi |

Sons of Bjartmar—Helgi, Sigurd, Vestgeir—uncles of Aud and Vestein.

Thorgrim, son of Thorstein, Thordis's first husband.

Bork, Thorgrim's brother, Thordis's second husband; called 'the stout'.

Asgerd, wife of Thorkell, Gisli's brother.

Thorkell, son of Eirik, farmer in Dyrafjord, Gisli's friend.

Thorkell, son of Thord, farmer in Dyrafjord, Gisli's friend; called 'the rich'.

Onund, farmer of Medaldal, Gisli's friend.

Geirmund
Gudrid, his sister } brought up by Gisli and Thorkell, his brother.

Thord, a slave in Gisli's service; called 'the coward'.

Ingjald, farmer in Hergilsey; said to be Gisli's cousin.

Gest, son of Oddleif, a wise man and possessed of prophetic powers; said to be related to the sons of Vestein.

Eyjolf, son of Thord, Bork's cousin and chief ally; called 'the grey'.

Saka-Stein
Thorodd } nephews of Bork.

Spying Helgi, a minion of Eyjolf's.

Thorgrim neb, a farmer in Haukadal, skilled in sorcery.

Audbjorg, a widow living in Haukadal, sister of Thorgrim neb and, like him, skilled in sorcery.

A Note on the Original Text

THE TEXT OF the story of Gisli followed in this translation is that
printed in the volume of *Vestfirðinga sögur*, edited by Björn K.
Þórólfsson in the series 'Íslenzk Fornrit' (volume vi, Reykjavík,
1943). This is a conservative text based on manuscript AM 556a
4to (Arnamagnæan Institute, University of Copenhagen), written
in the fifteenth century. Occasionally the readings of other manuscripts have been preferred in the translation, or some slight
rearrangements have been made, in places where there is such
confusion in the Icelandic text that the flow of the narrative is
disturbed. A comparison with the edition mentioned above will
show where this has been done and why.

Other texts of the *Gisla saga* are preserved in the fragmentary
manuscript AM 445c 4to, from the beginning of the fifteenth
century, and in eighteenth-century transcripts of a now lost
vellum. It used to be thought that these two forms of the text had
a common origin, which meant that their combined evidence had
no greater value than the single witness of AM 556a 4to in
establishing an original text. Recently, however, it has been
suggested that the two are in fact independent of each other. It
ought thus to be possible to reconstruct a more original text than
is found in any single manuscript, by preferring the readings of
any two manuscripts that are in agreement against a third. The
readings of AM 556a 4to would then not infrequently have to be
replaced by those of the other manuscripts. No such attempt to
produce a more original text has been made here, chiefly because
it could be done for only about two-fifths of the whole saga, the
extent of the fragmentary AM 445c 4to.

AM 556a 4to gives a reasonably intelligent version. It has
clearly been edited to some extent in its transmission and
received some minor additions. The fragmentary AM 445c 4to
tends to shorten the original text, while the version preserved in

the young transcripts has been expanded, especially at the beginning (chapters 1–4). One can form some impression of the character of the editor of the version here translated on the evidence of his palpable additions: a rather prosaic, orderly man, not without a certain heavy-handed humour. This sentence on p. 30, for example, must be ascribed to him: 'This fellow had as much sense as he had spirit, for he had none of either'; and the italicized words in these sentences: 'She went home, and was somewhat foolisher than before, *if that were possible* . . .' (p. 16); 'Gisli spoke a verse *which he should have kept to himself*' (p. 26). His phrasing is usually fuller and smoother than that of the other texts where they are in agreement, but it cannot be seen that he has essentially altered the matter and spirit of the saga. Even in such a sentence as that beginning 'I did not think I had deserved this from her . . .' (p. 28), which is probably also largely his work, he seems to be doing no more than emphasizing an aspect of Gisli's character that was already evident in the original story (cf. the Essay, p. 108).

A
Note on the Translation

MY FIRST INTENTION was to make a twentieth-century telling
of the saga that would read as though it were a novel. After
several attempts Peter Foote asked Ian Maxwell in Melbourne
to read the version we then had, and because of his criticisms I
decided to rewrite the translation from start to finish, following
the Icelandic as closely as I could. The version that came out
seemed livelier, subtler and more readable, slightly outlandish in
tone, the style directly geared to the telling of the story. I wrote
in twentieth-century words, however, and kept out archaisms,
which would have seemed quaint or remote. It seemed to me that
the 'otherness' of the Icelandic was best preserved by letting its
word-order and idiom, especially in the shifting of tenses, play
their part in the English too.

The verses posed a more difficult problem. Their metre, diction
and syntax are complex and artificial and their content is often
slight: their value as poetry seems not very high. Yet they contain
many of the keys of the story and, especially in this saga, their
artificiality set in the stern spareness of the narrative gives the
whole book a lyrical quality it would not otherwise have; many
of them, in context, are true lyrics. They cannot be directly
rendered in English, however; even a literal prose translation
could rarely be faithful to their twisted syntax, and it would have
to be heavily annotated on account of the allusiveness of the
diction. So I decided to follow the metre closely, use as much of
the imagery as could be fitted in, and give the sense of the
original without attempting direct translation.

The imagery is conventional. It is drawn from myths and
legends and chiefly takes the form of kennings, a Germanic kind
of poetic diction, which the scalds used in their own elaborate
way. Many of the kennings seem far-fetched to us, yet they have

associations which may make them rich and suggestive even to our ears. For instance, here is the story behind a kenning ('to pour the dwarfs' liquor', meaning 'to speak in poetry') which appears in two of Gisli's stanzas (pp. 40 and 55). It is translated from *Skáldskaparmál*, 'The Diction of Poetry', in Snorri's *Edda*, written about 1220.

'Where did the art come from that you call poetry?

Bragi replies: This is how it began—that the gods were on bad terms with the people who are called the Vanir. They held a peace meeting and made a truce by each of them going to a tub and spitting his spit in it. When they parted, the gods took it and did not want this symbol of the truce to be lost, so they made a man out of it. He is called Kvasir. He is so wise that no one asks him any question that he cannot answer. He travelled wide through the world to teach men lore. When he came to a feast that was being held by certain dwarfs, Fjalar and Galar, they called him aside for a private talk and killed him and let his blood run into two tubs and a cauldron; the cauldron is called Odrorir and the tubs are called Son and Bodn. They mixed honey with the blood and from it came the mead which if anyone drinks he becomes a scald or a learned man. The dwarfs told the gods that Kvasir had suffocated in his learning because nobody there knew enough to ask him questions. Then these dwarfs asked the giant Gilling and his wife to visit them. They asked Gilling to row out to sea with them, and when they were coming round the coast the dwarfs rowed on to a shoal and upset the boat. Gilling could not swim and he drowned, but the dwarfs righted the boat and rowed to land. They told his wife what had happened, and she took it badly and wailed loudly. Fjalar asked her whether it would ease her mind if she looked out to the place at sea where her husband had drowned, and she wanted to do that. Then he told his brother Galar to climb up over the doorway and drop a quern-stone on her head when she went out. He said he was fed up with her wail. Galar did so. When Suttung, Gilling's son, heard of this, he goes to the dwarfs and seizes them and takes them out to sea and puts them on a reef that flooded at high water. They beg for their lives, and offer by way of compensation for his father the precious mead, and this brings about a truce between them. Suttung takes the mead home and keeps it in the place called Hnitbjorg, and sets his daughter Gunnlod to guard it. From this we call the scald's art Kvasir's blood, or the dwarfs' drink, or the dwarfs' repletion, or some kind of liquid of Odrorir or Bodn or Son, or the ferry-boat of the dwarfs, because this mead ransomed them from the reef, or Suttung's mead, or the sea of Hnitbjorg.'

Some notes on the kennings that appear in the verse in this book are printed on pp. 61–3.

Bibliographical Note (1978)

Since 1963 the Royal Library, Copenhagen, has published an annual *Bibliography of Old Norse—Icelandic Studies*, edited by Hans Bekker-Nielsen. This invaluable publication provides full information about works of scholarship relating to *The Saga of Gisli*. There has been continued lively discussion of central problems: the interpretation of Gisli's character, the identity of Vestein's killer, the order of priority among the main redactions, and the saga's literary relationships.

The Saga of Gisli

I

WHEN THIS STORY begins, King Hakon, foster-son of Athelstan, was ruling over Norway, and it was near the end of his days. There was a man named Thorkell, who had the nickname skerauki; he lived in Surnadal, and was a chieftain by title. He had a wife whose name was Isgerd, and three children, all sons. One was named Ari, another Gisli, and the third Thorbjorn—he was the youngest—and they all grew up at home. There was a man by the name of Isi; he lived in the fjord which is called Fibuli, in Nordmøre; his wife was named Ingigerd and his daughter Ingibjorg. Ari, the son of Thorkell of Surnadal, asks for Ingibjorg's hand in marriage, and she was given to him with a large dowry. A bondservant named Kol came with her.

There was a man known as pale-faced Bjorn, who was a berserk; he went about the country challenging men to fight if they would not give in to his demands. He came during the winter to Thorkell of Surnadal's place. Ari, his son, was then in charge of the farm. Bjorn gives Ari two choices, whether he will rather fight with him on an island that lies near by in Surnadal, called Stokkaholm, or give over his wife to him. He chose at once, that he will rather fight than have shame come on him and his wife too. They were to meet after three days. Now the time comes round, they fight, and the outcome is that Ari falls and loses his life. It seems to Bjorn that he has won land and woman. Gisli says that he will rather lose his own life than let this come about, and he is bent on fighting Bjorn.

Then Ingibjorg had something to say: 'When I was married to Ari, it was not because I would not rather have been married to you. Kol, my bondservant, has a sword which is called Greyflank, and you must ask him to lend it to you; because with this sword it happens that whoever takes it into a fight wins.'

1

He asks the bondman for the sword, and the bondman made no small thing of lending it. Gisli got ready for the duel, they fight, and it turns out that Bjorn falls. Now it seemed to Gisli that he had won a great victory; and the story tells that he asks for Ingibjorg, for he did not want to lose a good woman from the family, and marries her; and he takes over all the property and becomes an important man. Then his father dies, and Gisli takes over his property as well. He had them all killed, who had been with Bjorn.

The bondman claimed back his sword, but Gisli will not give it up, and offers him money for it, but the bondman wants nothing but the sword itself; he gets it none the more for that. The bondman resents this and attacks Gisli and wounds him badly. Gisli hits back at the bondman's skull with Greyflank so hard that the sword broke, and the skull was broken, and both men die.

2

AFTER THIS Thorbjorn takes over all the property which had belonged to his father and two brothers. He lives in Surnadal, at Stokkar. He asks for the woman who was called Thora, Raud's daughter of Fridarey, and marries her. Their life together was happy, and before long they had children. Their daughter was named Thordis; she was their eldest child. Thorkell was the name of their eldest son, Gisli the second, and Ari the youngest, and they grew up at home. There were no more outstanding men to be found in the district of their age. Then Ari was taken as foster-son by Styrkar, his mother's brother, but Thorkell and Gisli stayed at home.

There was a man called Bard; he lived in Surnadal; he was a young man and had recently inherited his father's property. Another man called Kolbjorn lived at Hella in Surnadal; he was a young man and had newly come into his inheritance. Certain people said that Bard was seducing Thordis, Thorbjorn's daughter—she was both handsome and intelligent. This displeased Thorbjorn, and he said he thought that if Ari was at home things would not turn out well. Bard said that "the words of a weakling are worthless"—'and I shall go on as usual'.

2

Thorkell was friendly with Bard, and he was in with him in this, but the way his sister was going on with Bard angered Gisli as much as it did his father. One time, they say, Gisli joined Bard and Thorkell. He went as far as halfway to Grannaskeid—this is the name of the place where Bard lived—and then, when it was least expected, Gisli strikes Bard his death-blow. Thorkell was angry, and said that Gisli had done wrong, but Gisli told his brother to be calm—'and let us change swords, and you take the one that bites better'. He began to joke with him. Thorkell grows calm then, and sits down beside Bard. Gisli goes home and tells his father, and he was pleased. There was never full friendliness between the brothers again, and Thorkell did not accept the exchange of weapons, and he would not remain at home, but went to Holmgang-Skeggi, who lived on Saxa Island—he was a close kinsman of Bard—and stayed there.

He egged on Holmgang-Skeggi to avenge his kinsman, Bard, and marry Thordis. They went together to Stokkar in a party twenty strong; and when they came to the farmhouse Skeggi spoke to Thorbjorn of marriage ties—'and having your daughter Thordis as my wife'. But Thorbjorn would not let him have the girl. Kolbjorn was said to be courting Thordis. Skeggi thought that Kolbjorn was the cause of his not getting the marriage, and he goes to see him, and challenges him to fight on Saxa Island. Kolbjorn agrees that he will come, and said he would not be worthy of marrying Thordis if he has not the courage to fight Skeggi.

Thorkell and Skeggi went back to Saxa and awaited the meeting there with their twenty followers. And after three days Gisli went to see Kolbjorn, and asked if he was ready for the fight. Kolbjorn answers by asking if that is the way he must win her.

'Don't talk like that,' says Gisli.

Kolbjorn says: 'I feel as though I will not fight Skeggi to win her.'

Gisli calls him the worst kind of coward—'and you can come to shame altogether, but I shall go anyhow'.

He takes eleven men and goes to the island. Meanwhile Skeggi had come to the place, and he sets forth the duelling rules and challenges Kolbjorn by marking out the ring, but he says he does not see him there, nor anyone to take his place. Skeggi had a carpenter called Ref. He told Ref to make wooden figures of Gisli and Kolbjorn—'and have one stand close behind the

3

other; and the nastiness of that will always be there to shame them'.

Gisli heard this as he came through the trees, and he answers: 'Your men will have something more useful than that to do; and you can look here at a man who is not afraid to fight you.'

They go into the ring and fight, and each holds a shield to guard himself. Skeggi has a sword called Warflame, and he swings it at Gisli so that it makes a loud whistle; then says Skeggi:

> *Warflame whistled,*
> *Wild sport for Saxa.*

Gisli struck back at him with a halberd and took off the point of his shield and one of his legs, and he said:

> *Hack went the halberd,*
> *Hewed down Skeggi.*

Skeggi bought himself off from the duel and from then on went on a wooden leg. Thorkell went home with Gisli, his brother, and they were on good brotherly terms again, and Gisli came out of this fight a much greater man.

3

THE STORY MENTIONS two brothers, one named Einar and the other Arni, the sons of Skeggi of Saxa. They lived at Flydruness, north of the Trondheim district. They raised a troop of men in the spring and they went to Kolbjorn in Surnadal and offered him two choices, whether he would rather go with them and burn Thorbjorn and his sons in their house, or die right there. He decided that he would rather go.

They set out, sixty men in all, and came to Stokkar in the night and set fire to the buildings. All were asleep in one room, Thorbjorn and his sons and Thordis. There were two tubs of whey in the house. Gisli and his brother and father take two goatskins and dip them in the whey-tubs and damp the fire with them, and they put down the flames three times this way; then they succeeded in breaking a way through the wall and got out through it, ten of them together and, under cover of the smoke, they got up the mountainside beyond dog's bark. Twelve men were burnt in the house. The attackers thought they had burnt everybody.

Gisli and the others go on until they come to Styrkar's house in Fridarey, and there they call out men to help them, forty in all, and come without warning to Kolbjorn's house and burn him in it with eleven other men. They then sell their land and buy a ship —there were sixty of them in it—and sail away with all their belongings to the islands called Aesundir, and lie up there waiting to put to sea. Meanwhile forty of them set out from there in two boats, and go north to Flydruness. The brothers, Skeggi's two sons, had just started out with seven other men to collect their farm rents. Gisli's party turn on them and kill them all; Gisli killed three men and Thorkell two. After this they go to the farmstead and take away much booty. Gisli cut off Skeggi's head this time; he had been staying there with his sons.

4

THEY RETURN TO the ship and put to sea and are away from land for more than sixty days, and they come ashore in west Iceland on the south strand of the Dyrafjord, in the estuary of the river of Haukadal. There were two men who lived on opposite sides of the fjord, both named Thorkell. One of them lived at Saurar in Keldudal on the southern shore—this was Thorkell Eiriksson; the other lived on the north side, at Alvidra—he was called Thorkell the rich. Thorkell Eiriksson was the first man of standing to go to the ship and greet whey-Thorbjorn, who was called this after he had escaped by means of the whey. All land had been taken on both shores. Whey-Thorbjorn bought land on the southern shore at Saebol in Haukadal, and Gisli built a steading there, where they lived from then on.

A man called Bjartmar lived in at the head of Arnarfjord; his wife was called Thurid and she was the daughter of Hrafn of Ketilseyr in Dyrafjord; this Hrafn was the son of Dyri, the first settler in the fjord. They had children: their daughter's name was Hild—she was the eldest; their sons were Helgi, Sigurd and Vestgeir. Vestein was the name of a Norwegian who came to Iceland at the time of the settlement, and lodged with Bjartmar. He married Hild, Bjartmar's daughter. When they had been married not very long they had two children: Aud was the name of their daughter and Vestein of their son. Vestein Vesteinsson became a good seafarer and trader. However, he had a farm called Hest in Onundarfjord at this time in the story. His wife was called Gunnhild; their sons were Berg and Helgi.

Now after this whey-Thorbjorn dies, and then his wife, Thora. Gisli and his brother Thorkell take over the farm; and Thorbjorn and Thora were buried in a mound.

5

THERE WAS A man, Thorbjorn, who was called seal's crag. He lived in Talknafjord at Kvigandafell. His wife was named Thordis and his daughter Asgerd. Thorkell, Gisli's brother, asks for this woman and marries her; and Gisli married Vestein's sister, Aud. Now the brothers farm together in Haukadal.

One spring Thorkell the rich had to make the journey south to the Thing at Thorsness, and Gisli and Thorkell went with him. At Thorsness there lived then Thorstein cod-biter, who was the son of Thorolf Mostrarskegg; he was married to Thora, the daughter of Olaf Thorsteinsson: their children were a daughter, Thordis, and Thorgrim, and Bork the stout. Thorkell finished his business at the Thing. And after the Thing Thorstein invited Thorkell the rich and the brothers Gisli and Thorkell to his home, and gave them good gifts at parting; and they invited Thorstein's sons to come west and visit them at their Thing the following spring. Then they journey home. Next spring Thorstein's sons make the journey west with ten companions to Hvalseyr Thing, and there they meet Gisli and Thorkell, who invite them home from the Thing; but before that they were to go to a feast at the home of Thorkell the rich. After that they visit whey-Thorbjorn's sons and are well feasted there.

To Thorgrim the sister of Gisli and Thorkell seems handsome, and he asks for her hand, and she is betrothed to him and a bridal feast is held at once; the steading at Saebol is given with her as a dowry and Thorgrim moves west to live; but Bork remains at Thorsness, and with him live his nephews, Saka-Stein and Thorodd. Now Thorgrim farms at Saebol; and the sons of whey-Thorbjorn go to Holl and build a good steading there; and only a fence lies between the land of Holl and the land of Saebol. They farm there side by side and are good friends. Thorgrim has the rank of a *godi*, and he is a great source of strength to the brothers. They go together to the local Thing, one spring, with forty men, and all of them were dressed in coloured clothes. Vestein, Gisli's brother-in-law, was in the party, and all the men who had come out from Surnadal.

6

THERE WAS A man called Gest, who was the son of Oddleif; he had come to the Thing and stayed in the booth of Thorkell the rich. They sit and drink, the Surnadal men; but other men were in the court, for it was a Thing for hearing lawsuits. A man comes into the booth of the Haukadal men, a talkative fellow by the name of Arnor, and said: 'You are a fine lot, you Haukdalers—attending to nothing but the drink, and will not come to the court where your thing-men have cases to be heard—everyone thinks so, although I am the one to say it.'

Then Gisli said: 'Let us go to the court then; it may be that others are saying the same.'

They go to the court; and Thorgrim asks if any men need their support—'and there will be no holding back, so long as we are standing, in any help we promise'.

But Thorkell the rich replies: 'These cases amount to little that men have against each other here; we will tell you if we need you.'

Now word begins to go around about how showy these men are, and about their talk, how bold it is. Thorkell spoke to Gest: 'How long do you expect that the spirit and swagger of these Haukdalers will be so great?'

Gest answers: 'They will not all think alike in three summers, who are now in that party.'

Arnor was near by during this, and he bursts into the Haukdalers' booth and tells them what he has heard. Gisli says: 'These are somebody's real words he has told us, and let us see to it that his prophecy doesn't turn out right. I can think of a good thing to do, and that is to bind our friendship with stronger ties, and swear blood-brotherhood between the four of us.'

This seems a good answer. They go out to the spit of land

7

called Eyrarhvalsoddi and cut and raise up a long sod in the turf, leaving the two ends fast, and they set a spear with a damascened blade under it, so long-shafted that a man could just reach the rivets of the head with outstretched hand. All four should pass under, Thorgrim, Gisli, Thorkell and Vestein; and now they draw blood and let their blood run together in the earth which was scratched up under the sod, and mix it all together, earth and blood; and then they kneel and swear an oath, that each shall avenge the other as his brother, and they call all the gods to witness. But when they came to shake hands Thorgrim said: 'There is burden enough in this for me if I do it with these two, Thorkell and Gisli, my brothers-in-law; but I have no ties with Vestein'—and he draws back his hand.

'Then more of us will do the same,' says Gisli, and he too draws back his hand, 'for I will not bind myself to the man who will not bind himself to Vestein, my wife's brother.'

People thought this a serious thing. Gisli said then to Thorkell, his brother: 'It has gone as I thought it would; what we have just done will be of no use; and I think that fate will have its way over this.'

Men go home, now, from the Thing.

7

DURING THE summer it happened that a ship came to Dyrafjord, owned by two brothers, Norwegians; one was named Thorir and the other Thorarin, and they were men from the Oslofjord. Thorgrim rode to the ship and bought timber to the value of sixteen ounces of silver, and paid some of the price down and left some to be paid later. The traders then laid up their ship in the Sanda estuary and found lodgings for themselves. A man named Odd, the son of Orlyg, lived at Eyr in Skutilsfjord; he took the two brothers.

Thorgrim sends his son Thorodd to look over and count his timber, because he intends to fetch it home soon. Thorodd comes and looks over the timber, but the lot they were buying looks to him rather different from what Thorgrim had told him. He used hard words to the Norwegians; but they would not stand for this, and they attack him and kill him. Then the Norwegians go away from the ship after this work. They cross over Dyrafjord and take horse and make for their lodgings in Eyr; they journey all day and all night until they come to the dale which leads up out of Skutilsfjord, and here they eat breakfast and go to sleep.

Thorgrim is told the news and he sets out at once. He has himself ferried across the fjord and goes after them alone. He reaches them, where they were lying, and wakes Thorarin; he prods him with his spear-shaft. Thorarin springs up and tries to draw his sword, because he knew Thorgrim. But Thorgrim thrusts at him with his spear, and kills him. Now Thorir wakes, and he wants to avenge his companion. But Thorgrim thrusts his spear through him. The place is now called Breakfast Dale and Eastmen's Fall. Thorgrim returns home and becomes famous for this journey.

He stays on his farm over the winter. In the spring the brothers-in-law, Thorgrim and Thorkell, fit out the ship which had belonged to the Norwegians. These Norwegians had been great trouble-makers in Norway, and the country was no longer safe for them. Now Thorgrim and Thorkell make this ship ready and put to sea in it. This summer Vestein and Gisli also sail out, from Skeljavik in Steingrimsfjord. Both ships sail out to sea. Onund of Medaldal looks after Thorkell and Gisli's farm, and Saka-Stein, along with Thordis, looks after Saebol. At this time Harald Greycloak was ruling over Norway. Thorgrim and Thorkell bring their ship ashore in the north of Norway, and they soon fall in with the king and present themselves to him and pay their respects. He received them well, and they joined his sworn retainers and won generous rewards and honours.

Gisli and Vestein were at sea more than sixty days, and they ran ashore in early winter in Hordland in a gale of wind and snow during the night, and they smashed their ship, but saved their goods and men.

8

A MAN NAMED beard-Bjalfi had a trading-ship there. He was intending to sail south to Denmark. They ask him if they can buy a half share in his ship. He says he has heard that they are good men, and he gave them the half share, but they at once repay him with gifts worth more.

9

They voyage south to Denmark to the market town called Viborg, and stay the winter there with the man called Sigrhadd. The three of them, Vestein, Gisli and Bjalfi, were there; and they became good friends and exchanged gifts. Then early in the spring Bjalfi readied his ship to go to Iceland. There was a man by the name of Sigurd, a trading partner of Vestein, Norwegian by birth, who was out west in England. He sent word to Vestein that he wanted to close the partnership because he no longer needed Vestein's money. So Vestein asks leave to go and settle up with him.

'Then you must promise that you will never go from Iceland, if you come safely back, unless I let you.'

Vestein says yes to this.

One morning Gisli gets up and goes to the smithy. He was the handiest of men and skilled in everything. He made a coin which weighed not less than an ounce, and riveted it together with twenty studs in it, ten in each half, so that the coin seemed whole if it was put together, and yet it could be separated into two parts. The story goes that he takes the coin apart and puts one piece in Vestein's hand and tells him to keep it as a token between them —'and we must each send his part to the other only if it is a matter of life and death. Yet my mind tells me that we will need to send them, though we may not meet again'.

Vestein sails west to England—and Gisli and Bjalfi to Norway, and then in the summer to Iceland. They had got much money and reputation; they ended their partnership on good terms, and Bjalfi bought the half share in the ship back from Gisli. Then Gisli journeys west to Dyrafjord in a merchant ship, with eleven men.

9

THORGRIM AND THORKELL ready their ship in another place and return to Iceland, to the river-mouth in Haukadal in Dyrafjord, on the same day as Gisli had already sailed in on the merchant ship. They soon meet, and a joyful meeting it is; and then they go to their homes. Thorgrim and Thorkell had prospered on their voyage as well.

Thorkell was a vain man, and did not work on the farm, but

Gisli worked night and day. So it happened on a day of good weather that Gisli sent all the men out haymaking, except Thorkell; he was the only man left at home at the farm, and he was lying down in the hall after his morning meal. The hall was a hundred and fifty feet long and sixty feet wide; on its south-west side stood the bower of Aud and Asgerd, and they were sitting there and sewing. When Thorkell wakes up he goes toward the bower, because he heard voices coming from there, and he lies down on the nearest side. Now Asgerd speaks: 'Do something for me, Aud. Cut out a shirt for me, for my husband Thorkell.'

'I could not do it better than you,' says Aud, 'and you would not ask me if you had to make a shirt for my brother Vestein.'

'That is another story,' says Asgerd; 'and I shall feel like that for a while.'

'It is something I have known about for a long time,' says Aud. 'Let us not talk about it any more.'

'Nothing seems wrong to me', says Asgerd, 'if I think well of Vestein; I have been told that you and Thorgrim often met before you were married to Gisli.'

'No blame came of that,' says Aud, 'because I have had nothing to do with a man since I married Gisli, from which there might come blame; and now we will stop this talk.'

But Thorkell hears everything they had said, and he speaks up now that they have left off:

> *'Hear a great marvel,*
> *Hear of manslaughter,*
> *Hear a great matter,*
> *Hear of a man's death—*

of one man, or more,' and he goes in.

Then Aud speaks. 'Trouble often comes from women's talk, and perhaps the trouble from ours will be the worst kind. We must decide what to do.'

'I have a plan for myself,' says Asgerd, 'which will work well enough; but I don't know the best thing for you.'

'What is your plan?' asked Aud.

'Put my arms round Thorkell's neck when we come to bed— and he will forgive me for this—and then tell him it is all a lie.'

'That will not be enough to count on, by itself,' said Aud.

'What will you do?' asked Asgerd.

'Tell my husband Gisli everything that I can't otherwise talk about or decide.'

11

In the evening Gisli comes in from work. Usually Thorkell would thank his brother for what he has done, but now he is glum and said not a word. Gisli asks him whether he is feeling all right.

'I am not ill,' says Thorkell; 'but this is worse than illness.'

'Have I done anything,' says Gisli, 'that has offended you?'

'Not in any way,' says Thorkell. 'You will know all about it, though perhaps not till later.'

They each go about their affairs, and there was no more talk between them.

Thorkell eats little food that evening, and he is the first man to go to bed. And when he had settled down Asgerd comes and lifts the blanket and makes to lie beside him. Then Thorkell broke his silence: 'I do not mean to have you lie here tonight, nor for many nights.'

Asgerd speaks. 'Why have you changed so suddenly? What is the matter here?' she asks.

Thorkell says: 'We both know now what the reason is, though it was kept from me for a long while; and your reputation will be no better if I speak plainer.'

She replies: 'You may think what you like about it, but I will not quarrel long over the bed with you; and you have two things to choose from. One is that you take me in and behave as though nothing has happened; otherwise I shall call witnesses at once, and declare my divorce from you, and I will have my father claim back my price and my dowry; and if this is your choice you will never have my bed company again.'

Thorkell was quiet then, and after a while he said: 'I advise you to do whichever you like; but I will not keep you out of bed all night.'

She immediately showed what she most wanted and got straight into bed. They had not been side by side for long before they settled the matter between them as though nothing had happened.

Aud went into bed with Gisli, and she tells him of the talk she has had with Asgerd, and asks him not to be angry with her; and asked him to do something about it, if he could see anything good to be done.

'I can see nothing to be done about it,' he said, 'that will help; and yet I cannot blame you, for "Fate's words will be spoken by someone", and what is to follow, will follow.'

10

THE YEAR PASSES by and moving-days come round. Now Thorkell asks his brother Gisli to talk with him, and said: 'It has come about, brother,' he says, 'that I have something of a notion and a mood to change the way I live; and it goes this way, that I want us to divide our property, and I will set up house with Thorgrim, my brother-in-law.'

Gisli answers: 'What belongs to brothers is best seen together; it would certainly please me to leave things as they are, and not split anything up.'

'We cannot go on this way any longer,' says Thorkell, 'house-holding together, because a great wrong comes out of it, since you always have the work and trouble of seeing to the farm, and I never lift a hand to anything useful.'

'Do not find any fault with that,' says Gisli, 'as long as I have nothing to say about it. We have been through both sorts of times, when things were well between us and when things were bad.'

'It does not matter what is said about it; the property must certainly be divided, and because I am the one to ask for the division, you shall have the homestead and land and I shall have the cash.'

'If there is nothing else for it but to separate, then you do one or the other—for I do not mind which I do—either divide or choose.'

It was settled that Gisli did the dividing, and Thorkell chose the cash and Gisli had the land. They also divided the dependants, who were two children; the boy was called Geirmund and the girl Gudrid, and she stayed with Gisli and Geirmund went with Thorkell. Thorkell went to Thorgrim, his brother-in-law, and lived with him; and Gisli then had the farm, and no such loss had been suffered that the farm was any the worse for it.

The summer now passes in this way, and the Winter Nights come. It was the custom of many men to welcome winter in those days, and hold feasts and winter night sacrifices, but Gisli no longer sacrificed since his stay at Viborg in Denmark, though he still held feasts as before, and did everything with magnificence. Now he makes preparations for a great feast, when the time comes that was just spoken of, and he asks to the feast the two

13

namesakes, Thorkell Eiriksson and Thorkell the rich, and Aud's kinsmen, the sons of Bjartmar, and many other friends and acquaintances. And on the day when the guests arrive Aud speaks: 'It is true to say that one man seems missing to me, who I wish might be here.'

'Who is that?' asked Gisli.

'It is my brother Vestein; I would like him to enjoy this feast here with us.'

Gisli said: 'I think differently about it, because I would willingly give money to have him not come here now.'

And with this their talk comes to an end.

I I

THERE WAS A man by the name of Thorgrim, who was called Thorgrim neb. He lived at Neb's steading on the east side of the Haukadal river. He was full of sorcery and witchcraft, and he was as much a wizard as could be. Thorgrim and Thorkell invited him to come to their place because they too were having a feast. Thorgrim neb was skilful with iron, and the story says that both Thorgrims and Thorkell go to the smithy and shut themselves in. The bits of Greyflank are brought out—they had fallen to Thorkell's lot when the brothers split up their property—and Thorgrim neb makes a spear out of them, and the work was all done by evening; there was damascening in the blade, and a short handle fitted to it, about eight inches long. So much for them.

The story now goes that Onund of Medaldal came to the feast at Gisli's, and he took him aside and said that Vestein had come back to Iceland—'and he can be expected here'. Gisli moves at once and calls his housemen, Hallvard and Havard, and told them to go north to Onundarfjord and meet Vestein—'and take him my greeting, and tell him at the same time that he is to stay at home until I visit him, and he is not to come to the feast in Haukadal'. And he puts into their hands a knotted kerchief, and the half coin was in it as a token, in case he should not believe their story. They go then, and take a boat from Haukadal and row to Laekjaross and come ashore and call on the farmer who lived there at Bersi's steading; he was called Bersi. They give him a message from Gisli that he is to lend them two horses which he had, called the Bandvettir, the swiftest in the fjords. He lends them the horses, and they ride until they come to Mosvellir, and from there in towards Hest. Meanwhile Vestein sets out from home, and it happens that he rides below the sandhill at Mosvellir as the brothers are riding along the top, and so they pass by and miss each other.

12

THERE WAS A man named Thorvard, who lived at Holt. His housemen had fought over some work and struck each other with scythes, and both were wounded. Vestein comes by and stops the fight, and does it in such a way that the men become friends again and each is satisfied; then he rides out towards Dyrafjord with his two Norwegian companions.

But Hallvard and Havard come in to Hest and hear that in fact Vestein has already set out—they turn and ride after him at their hardest. And when they come to Mosvellir they see men riding in the middle of the valley, but there was a hill between them; they ride now into Bjarnardal and come to Arnkelsbrekka; there both horses founder. They run from the horses then, and shout. Vestein and his men hear them now; they had come as far as Gemlufall Moor, and they wait there until they come up and give their message—they hand over the coin which Gisli has sent for him. He takes out the other half of the coin from his money belt and turns very red as he looks at it.

'You speak the truth,' he says, 'and I should have turned back if you had met me sooner, but now the streams all run towards Dyrafjord and I shall ride there; and in any case I want to. The Norwegians will turn back. But you get on by boat,' says Vestein, 'and tell Gisli and my sister of my coming.'

They go home and tell Gisli. He answers: 'That is how it must be, then.'

Vestein goes on to Gemlufall, to Luta, his kinswoman, and she has him ferried across the fjord and said to him: 'Vestein,' she said, 'be wary for yourself; there is need of it.' He is taken over to Thingeyr; a man lived there then who was called Thorvald spark. Vestein goes to his house, and Thorvald lends him his horse, but Vestein kept his own saddle gear and he rides off with his bridle jingling. Thorvald rides with him to Sandaoss and offers to stay with him all the way to Gisli's. He said there was no need for it.

'Much has changed in Haukadal,' said Thorvald; 'be wary for yourself.' Then they part.

Vestein rides now till he comes into Haukadal, and there was bright weather there, and moonlight. At Thorgrim's they were bringing in the cattle, Geirmund and a woman called Rannveig; she pens the cattle and he drives them in to her. Vestein rides up across the field and Geirmund comes over to him.

Geirmund spoke. 'Do not come in here to Saebol but go on to Gisli's, and be wary for yourself.'

Rannveig had come out of the cattle shed, and she looks at the man and thinks she knows him, and when the cattle have been brought in they argue about the man, who he was, and so go to the house. Thorgrim and the others are sitting by the fire, and Thorgrim asks if they have seen or met anybody, or what are they arguing about.

'I thought I recognized Vestein coming here,' said Rannveig, 'and he was in a blue cape and he had a spear in his hand, and he rode with a jingling bridle.'

'And what do you say, Geirmund?'

'I could hardly see him; but I thought he was one of Onund's housemen from Medaldal, and he was wearing Gisli's cape, and he was using Onund's saddle gear, and he had a fishing spear in his hand with a prong at the top.'

'One of you must be lying,' said Thorgrim. 'You go over to Holl, Rannveig, and see what is going on.'

She went over and came to the door when the men had arrived for the drinking. Gisli was standing in the doorway, and he spoke to her and asked her to come in. She said she should be going home—'but I should like to speak to the girl, Gudrid'.

Gisli calls her, but nothing to any purpose came of it.

'Where is Aud, your wife?' she says.

'Here she is,' says Gisli. She goes out and asked what she wanted. She replied that it was only a small matter, but nothing came of it. Gisli told her to do one or the other, come in or go home. She went home, and was somewhat foolisher than before, if that were possible, and had no news to tell.

In the morning Vestein had two bags brought to him with goods in them, which the brothers, Hallvard and Havard, had carried for him. He took out a tapestry ninety feet long, a head-dress made of a piece of stuff thirty feet long with three gold

16

strands woven along its length, and three basins decorated with gold. He took these and offered them to his sister and Gisli and to Thorkell, his oath-brother, if he would accept. Gisli goes to Saebol with the two Thorkells to his brother Thorkell. Gisli says that Vestein has come, and he has given them gifts to share, and he shows them to him and asks him to have whatever he chooses.

Thorkell answers: 'It would be more fitting if you were to take all, and I will not accept the gifts: any return for them from me is not very likely.' And he will not take them at all.

Gisli goes home now, and it seems to him that everything is tending the same way.

13

NOW A STRANGE thing happens at Holl that Gisli sleeps badly two nights together, and they ask him what he has dreamed. He will not tell his dreams. Then comes the third night and they go to bed, and when they have been asleep so hard a squall of wind hits the house that it takes all the thatch from one side. With this so much water fell from the sky that it was something unheard of, and the buildings let in the rain, as might be expected, when the thatch shifted. Gisli sprang up quickly and calls his men to save the hay.

Gisli had a thrall whose name was Thord, and he was nick-named the coward. The thrall stayed in the house, but Gisli, and nearly all the other men, went to see to the haystacks. Vestein offered to go with him, but Gisli will not have it. And now, when the roof started leaking worse, the sister and brother turn their beds lengthwise down the room; everyone else had left the room except only these two. Then someone comes in a little before dawn, quietly, and goes over to where Vestein is lying. He had woken up then. The first thing he knows is that a spear is thrust into his breast and right through him.

When Vestein took the blow, then he spoke this: 'A heart thrust!' he said, and then the man went out. Vestein tried to stand up; but he fell beside the bed, dead.

Aud wakes up now, and calls to Thord the coward and tells him to take the weapon from the wound. It was said then that whoever pulled the weapon from a wound would be bound to take revenge; it was called secret manslaughter and not murder when the weapon was left in a death wound. Thord was so fearful of corpses that he did not dare go near one. Gisli came in then and saw what had happened, and he told Thord to be still. He took the spear from the wound himself and threw it, all bloody, into a chest, and let nobody see. Then he sat on the edge of the bed.

He had Vestein's body got ready for burial, as they used to do it in those times. Vestein's death brought great grief both to Gisli and to other men. Gisli spoke to Gudrid, his foster-daughter. 'You shall go to Saebol and see what they are doing there; I am sending you on this errand because I have greatest faith in you in this as in other things, and be sure you can tell me what they are doing there.'

She goes, and comes to Saebol. They were up and sitting armed, the two Thorgrims and Thorkell. When she came in she was not greeted quickly, for the people there mostly had little to say for themselves. However, Thorgrim asks her for her news. She told of Vestein's death, or murder.

Thorkell answers: 'That would have seemed news to us at one time.'

'A man is there lost,' says Thorgrim, 'to whom we are all bound to show respect, and we are bound to give him burial with the greatest honour, and build a mound for him; and it is true to say that such a man is a great loss. You may also tell Gisli that we shall come today.'

She goes home and tells Gisli that Thorgrim sat with his helmet and sword and fully armed, and Thorgrim neb had a timber-axe in his hand, and Thorkell had his sword and it was drawn a hand's breadth—'and all the men were up and some were armed'.

'That was to be expected,' says Gisli.

14

GISLI NOW PREPARES, with all his men, to bury Vestein in the sandhill that stands beside the rush-pond below Saebol. And when Gisli was on his way Thorgrim and Thorkell and Thorgrim neb came with a large company of men to the mound-making. They did everything for Vestein as the ways then were, and then Thorgrim went to Gisli and spoke. 'It is a custom,' he says, 'to tie Hel-shoes on men which they should walk in to Valhall, and I shall do that for Vestein.' And when he had done so he said: 'I do not know how to tie Hel-shoes, if these come loose.'

After this they sit down by the mound and talk, and they agree that it is unlikely that anyone will know who has done this crime. Thorkell asked Gisli: 'How does Aud take the death of her brother? Does she weep much?'

'You will be thinking you know the answer to that,' says Gisli. 'It is heavy for her, and she takes it as a great loss.'

'I dreamt a dream,' says Gisli, 'the night before last and again last night, and I shall not say from the dreams who did the killing, although they point to that. I dreamt the night before last that out of a certain house slid a viper, and it stung Vestein to death. The next night I dreamt that a wolf ran out of the same house and bit Vestein to death. And I have not told either dream before now because I wanted nobody to interpret them.' Then he spoke a verse:

> '*Fearful nor dark forethought*
> *For Vestein oppressed me,*
> *Now I ask no third such*
> *Nightmare, come to fright me.*
> *Sat we on the settles,*
> *Sigrhadd's, mead-gladdened;*
> *Menace of man's envy*
> *Marred not then our heart joy.*'

Thorkell asked then: 'How does Aud take the death of her brother? Does she weep much?'

'You keep asking this, brother,' says Gisli, 'and you have a great curiosity to know.' Gisli spoke a verse:

> '*Carried under kerchief*
> *Keeps she in sleep's cisterns*
> *Surly drops of sorrow,*
> *Storm of cheek in secret.*
> *Oak of herbs from aching*
> *Eyes, from grief's high places,*
> *Has felt the salt dewfall,*
> *For her brother mourning.*'

And again he spoke:

> '*Sorrow, joy's dour slayer,*
> *Sways her twigs of hazel—*

19

Eye-lashes, all heavy;
Utter they grief's nut fruits.
Picks the snake-plot goddess
Pity's fruit from bitter
Sight twigs, yet secretly
Summons this scald's comfort.'

The brothers go back to the house now, together. Thorkell spoke. 'These have been heavy tidings, and they will have been somewhat more grievous to you than to us; nevertheless, "a man is his own company for most of the way". I hope that you will not make so much of this that men become suspicious; I would like us to begin sports and be on as good terms as we ever have been before.'

'That is well spoken,' says Gisli, 'and I agree willingly, but on this condition, that if something happens to you in your lifetime that seems as much to you as this seems to me, then you will promise to carry on with the same understanding as you are now asking of me.'

Thorkell agrees.

Then they go into the house and hold Vestein's funeral feast. And when that has been drunk, they each go home, and everything was quiet again.

15

THEY BEGAN THE games as though nothing had happened. The brothers-in-law, Gisli and Thorgrim, played against each other oftenest, and the watchers could not decide which was stronger, though most of them thought that Gisli was. They played the ball-game on the ice of the rush-pond, and there was always a crowd. One day, when there was a very big crowd, Gisli called on them to divide up evenly for a game.

'An even division is what we want,' says Thorkell, 'and furthermore, we wish that you would not spare anything against Thorgrim; because word is going round that you are sparing yourself; but I should gladly see you win the full honour, if you are the stronger.'

'He and I have not fought it out yet,' says Gisli, 'but perhaps the time is coming when we shall.'

20

They play a game, and Thorgrim is outmatched—Gisli throws him, and the ball rolls out of bounds. Gisli tries to go after it, but Thorgrim holds him and does not let him get it. Then Gisli throws Thorgrim so hard that he can do nothing to save himself, and his knees are skinned and the blood spurts from his nose; and the flesh is torn from his knees. Thorgrim stood up slowly; he turned to Vestein's grave mound and spoke:

> *Spear in the wound sharply*
> *Sang. I feel no anguish.*

Gisli picked up the ball on the run and pitched it between Thorgrim's shoulders, so that he fell forward; then Gisli spoke:

> *Ball on the broad shoulder*
> *Banged. I feel no anguish.*

Thorkell sprang up and spoke: 'Now it can be seen who is strongest or the best in action, and let us stop now.' And so they did. The games were not played any more, and summer came on, and there was some coldness now between Thorgrim and Gisli.

Thorgrim decided to give an autumn feast on the eve of the winter season, and to welcome winter and make a sacrifice to Frey, and he invites his brother Bork, and Eyjolf Thordsson and many other important men. Gisli also makes ready a feast and invites his wife's kinsmen from Arnarfjord, and the two Thorkells, and no fewer than sixty men were expected at Gisli's. There was to be drinking at both houses, and the floors at Saebol were strewn with rushes from the rush-pond.

When Thorgrim and his people were making preparations, and were ready to hang the hall with tapestries, and the guests were expected that evening, then Thorgrim spoke to Thorkell: 'What we need here are the fine hangings that Vestein wanted to give you. It seems to me that there is a great difference between owning them outright and never using them at all; and now I want you to have them sent for.'

Thorkell answers: '"He knows all who knows when to stop", and I shall not send for them.'

'I shall do it, then,' said Thorgrim, and he told Geirmund to go.

Geirmund answers: 'I will do some work, but I have no taste for this errand.'

Thorgrim goes to him and strikes him a hard blow and said: 'Go now, then, if it seems better to you.'

'I shall go now,' he said, 'though now it seems worse; but you

21

can be sure that I shall be willing to give you the filly of the foal you have given me, and you will not be underpaid at that.'

Then he goes. And when he comes there Gisli and Aud are getting ready to hang the tapestries. Geirmund gave them his message and told them everything that had happened.

'What is your wish, Aud? Shall we lend the tapestries?' said Gisli.

'You do not ask because you do not know, that I wish them neither this favour nor any other that might do them honour.'

'Was it my brother Thorkell's wish?' said Gisli.

'He thought well of my coming for them.'

'That is good enough,' said Gisli, and he comes on the way with Geirmund and gives him the hangings. Gisli goes with him as far as the fence and speaks: 'Now it is this way—I think I have made good your errand, and I want you to be helpful in something that is important to me, for "a gift always looks to a return", you know, and I want you to slide back the bolts on three doors this evening; and you might remember how you were sent on this errand.'

Geirmund answers: 'Will your brother Thorkell be in danger?'

'In no danger,' says Gisli.

'It will be put on the right road, then,' says Geirmund.

And when he comes back home he throws down the hangings. Then Thorkell speaks: 'Gisli is not like other men for his patience, and he has bettered us.'

'These are what we need,' says Thorgrim, and they put up the hangings.

Then in the evening the guests come. And the weather thickens; after dark the snow falls in windless air and covers all the paths.

16

BORK AND EYJOLF come in the evening with sixty men; there were a hundred and twenty men altogether at Saebol, and half that number at Gisli's. They started the drinking during the evening, and then they went to bed and slept. Gisli spoke to Aud, his wife: 'I have not fed his horse for Thorkell the rich. Come with me and lock the door after me, and stay awake while I go out, and unlock the door for me again when I come back.'

He takes the spear Greyflank from the chest, and he is wearing a blue cape over his shirt and linen under-breeches, and he goes now to the stream which runs between the two steadings, and from which water was taken for both. He goes by the path to the stream, and then wades down the stream to the path which led to the other house. Gisli knew the lay-out at Saebol because he had put up the buildings; there was a way in through the byre. This is where he goes; thirty cows were stalled on either side; he ties the cows' tails together and closes the byre, and fixes the door in such a way that it may not be opened from the other side. Then he goes to the dwelling-house; and Geirmund had done his work, because the doors were not barred. He goes in and shuts the door after him, in the way it had been closed up during the evening.

Now he takes his time over everything. After shutting the door he stands and listens to hear if anyone is awake, and he finds that all are asleep. There were three lights in the room. He takes sedge from the floor and twists it together; then he throws it on one of the lights, and it goes out. He stands again and waits, in case anyone wakes up, but he hears nothing. He takes another twist of sedge and throws it on the nearest light and puts it out. Then he knows that not all are asleep, because he sees that a young man's hand reaches for the third light, and pulls the lamp down and snuffs it. Now he goes farther into the room to the bed closet where Thorgrim slept, and his sister, and the door was ajar, and they are both in bed. He goes up and gropes about inside and puts his hand on his sister's breast; she was sleeping next the outside.

Then Thordis spoke. 'Why is your hand so cold, Thorgrim?' and she wakes him.

Thorgrim asked: 'Do you want me to turn your way?' She thought he had put his arm over her.

Gisli waits yet for a while, and warms his hand in his shirt, and they both go to sleep; then he takes hold of Thorgrim gently, so that he wakes up. He thought that Thordis had roused him, and he turned to her. Gisli pulls back the covers with one hand, and with the other he thrusts Greyflank into Thorgrim so that it goes through him and sticks in the bed. Then Thordis calls out and says: 'Wake up, men in the room! Thorgrim is killed, my husband!'

Gisli turns away quickly towards the byre and goes out as he had intended, and makes the door fast behind him; he goes home then by the same way as he had come, and his tracks could not be seen. Aud unlocks the door for him when he comes home, and he goes to bed and behaves as though nothing has happened, and as though he has done nothing. But the men were still full of drink at Saebol and did not know what ought to be done; this caught them unawares, and because of this nothing was done that was either fitting or useful.

17

EYJOLF SPOKE: 'Big and bad things have happened, and these people are stupid who are here. I think the thing to do is to light the lamps and guard the doors, so that the man who has done the killing cannot get away.'

And so it was done. People think, when they cannot find him, that it must perhaps be someone in the house who has done the work. Time passes on and daylight comes. They took Thorgrim's body and pulled the spear out and prepared him for burial, and sixty men stayed there, while the other sixty set out for Gisli's place, at Holl. Thord the coward was outside, and when he sees the crowd of men, he runs in and says that a whole army is coming to the house, and he is in quite a flurry.

'That is well, then,' says Gisli, and he speaks a verse:

> ' Fell I not nor failed at
> Fierce words, but my piercing
> Blade mouth gave forth bloody
> Bane speech, its harsh teaching.
> Sole, I watch in silence,
> Seeing this loud people:
> While the ship-tree welters
> Worried shouts bestir them.'

Now they come to the house, Thorkell and Eyjolf; they go to the bed-closet which Gisli and his wife slept in, and Thorkell, Gisli's brother, goes ahead into the closet and sees where Gisli's shoes lie, frozen and all caked with snow; he pushes them under the foot-board so that other men will not see them. Then Gisli greets them and asks for their news. Big and bad news Thorkell tells him, and he asks Gisli if he knows what might lie behind it, and what should be done about it.

'Big and bad deeds follow one another closely,' says Gisli. 'We

24

will offer to help bury Thorgrim, for you have a right to expect that of us, and it is fitting that we do it honourably.'

They accept this offer, and they all go together to Saebol for the mound-making, and lay Thorgrim in a boat. Now they heap up the mound according to the old ways, and when it is ready to be closed, Gisli goes to the river-mouth and takes up a stone, so big as to be called a boulder, and puts it in the boat, and every timber seemed nearly to give way with it, and the boat creaked mightily, and he said: 'I cannot make fast a boat, if the weather moves this one.'

Some men said that this did not seem much unlike what Thorgrim had done with Vestein when he spoke about the Hel-shoes.

Now they go home from the burial. Gisli spoke to his brother, Thorkell: 'I think you owe it to me, brother, to keep things as friendly between us now as they have been, at their best; and let us start up the games.'

Thorkell readily agrees. And now each party go to their houses. Gisli has not a few men for company, but the feasting comes to an end, and Gisli sends off his guests with good gifts.

18

NOW THORGRIM'S wake is drunk, and Bork gives good gifts, for friendship's sake, to many men. The next thing that happens is that Bork pays Thorgrim neb to work a spell, that there should be no help for the man who had killed Thorgrim, however much men might want to give it to him, and there should be no rest for him in the country. He was given a nine-year-old ox for the curse. He goes to work on it at once, and makes himself a scaffold and works this magic with all its obscenity and devilry.

There was something else that seemed to have a strange meaning, that snow never stayed on the south-west side of Thorgrim's mound, and it did not freeze there; and men explained this by saying that he must have been so favoured by Frey for his sacrifices that the god was unwilling to have frost come between them. This went on through the winter while the brothers held their games there.

Bork moves into the house with Thordis, and marries her. She was pregnant at the time, and she gives birth to a son, and he is sprinkled with water and named Thorgrim at first, after his father; but as he grew up they found that he was moody and unruly, so they changed his name and called him Snorri.

Bork lived there over the winter and joined in the games. A woman named Audbjorg lived in the upper part of the valley at Annmarkastadir. She was the sister of Thorgrim neb. Her husband had been Thorkell, who was nicknamed the blemished. Her son's name was Thorstein; he was one of the strongest at the games, after Gisli. Gisli and Thorstein were always together against Bork and Thorkell. One day a great many people came to see the games, because many were curious to watch the play and to find out who was the strongest, or most skilful. And it happened, as in other places everywhere, that there was greater keenness among the players when there were more watchers. It is said that Bork had failed against Thorstein all day, and at last he grew angry and snapped Thorstein's bat for him, and Thorstein threw him and stretched him out on the ice. When Gisli sees this, he told him to play with all his might against Bork—'and I will change bats with you'. And so they did. Gisli sits down and goes to work on the bat, facing Thorgrim's mound; there was snow on the ground, and the women were sitting up on the slope, his sister Thordis and many others. Gisli spoke a verse which he should have kept to himself:

> 'Giant-bane Grim's grave mound,
> Grows thin shoots, unfrozen;
> God of war-blade gleaming
> Gained, by me, pain's ending.
> Wearer of grim war mask
> Wields at last his field plot;
> Him, for land who hungered,
> Halled earth made I swallow.'

Thordis got the verse by heart from the one hearing, and goes home, and by then she has worked out its meaning. They break up the games now, and Thorstein returns home.

There was a man by the name of Thorgeir, who was called heathcock; his farm was called Heathcock's steading. Another man, whose name was Berg, was called shortleg, and his farm was called Shortleg's marshland; it was east of the river. And now, as people are going home, Thorstein and Berg talk over the games and end by quarrelling; for Berg favours Bork and Thorstein argues against him, and Berg hits Thorstein a blow with the back of his axe-head. But Thorgeir comes between them and hinders Thorstein from revenging the blow.

Thorstein goes home to Audbjorg, his mother; she binds up his wound and grumbles about what has happened to him. The old woman gets no sleep that night, she is so fidgety. The weather was cold outside, and still and cloudless. She goes withershins about the house a few times and sniffs in all directions, with her nostrils lifted. And as she was doing these things the weather began to change, and there came a heavy, drifting snowstorm, and after that a thaw; a flood broke out on the mountainside and an avalanche rolled on to Berg's steading, and twelve men were killed there. The marks of the rock-fall may be seen to this day.

19

THORSTEIN GOES TO Gisli, and Gisli gives him shelter, and he gets away southward to Borgarfjord and goes abroad from there. And when Bork heard of the disaster at Berg's, he goes up to Annmarkastadir and has Audbjorg seized and he takes her out to Saltness and stones her to death. And when this has happened Gisli sets out and comes to Nefsstadir and catches Thorgrim neb and takes him out to Saltness, where a bag is put over his head and he is stoned to death, and then buried under a heap of stones beside his sister Audbjorg, on the ridge between Haukadal and Medaldal.

Things are quiet now, and the spring passes on. Bork goes south to Thorsness, meaning to live there, and it seems to him that his move westward has brought him no honour—he had lost such a man as Thorgrim was, and had got no redress. He makes ready for his move, and sets his house in order, and fixes his plans, for he means to make a second trip after his goods and his wife. Thorkell, Gisli's brother, also made up his mind to move, and sets out with Bork, his brother-in-law.

The story tells now that Thordis, daughter of whey-Thorbjorn, Bork's wife and Gisli's sister, went some distance on the way with her husband. Bork spoke: 'Now I want you to tell me why you were so moody last fall when we broke up the games, for you promised to tell me before I went away.' They have now come to Thorgrim's grave-mound when they begin this talk. She puts her foot in front of her and says she will go no farther; then she tells him what Gisli said when he looked at Thorgrim's mound and she recites the verse to him.

. 'And I think,' she says, 'that you need search no farther over Thorgrim's death, and a case against him will be rightly brought.'

At this Bork becomes very angry and said: 'I will turn back now and kill Gisli, and there is no sense in lingering.'

But Thorkell says he cannot agree to that. 'I am not sure how much truth there is in what Thordis has told us; it seems to me just as likely there may be nothing in it at all, and "women's counsels are often cold".'

So they ride on their way—as Thorkell has persuaded them—until they come to Sandaoss, and there they dismount and bait their horses. Bork was in a silent mood, and Thorkell said that he wanted to see his friend Onund. He rides off straightway, so hard that he is quickly out of sight. Then he swings round and goes to Holl and tells Gisli what has happened, that Thordis has now opened up the case, and found the meaning of his verse— 'and you must now make up your mind that it has come out into the open'. Gisli was silent, and then he spoke a verse:

> ' *Wife-veil-hearted wavering*
> *Warped to miss, my sister,*
> *Gjuki's daughter's great heart,*
> *Gudrun's soul, stern moody.*
> *Brooding wrath for brothers*
> *Bent her mood to vengeance;*
> *Heart's cause for her husband*
> *Held she not, but felled him.*

'I did not think I had deserved this from her, because I think I have shown more than once that her honour was as important to me as my own; sometimes I have put my life in danger for her sake, and now she has given me death's word. And I should like to know, brother, what I can look for from you, in your position, seeing what I have done.'

'Warning, if men are trying to kill you, but I will not give you protection that may bring a case against me. I think it a great wrong done to me that my kinsman Thorgrim has been killed, my partner and my good friend.'

'Was it to be expected that such a man as Vestein would be left unavenged? And I would not answer you as you have now answered me, nor act as you say you will.'

They part. Thorkell returns to Bork and they go on south to Thorsness, and Bork puts his house in order; and Thorkell buys land on Bardastrand, the farm that is called Hvamm. Then the summoning-days come round and Bork rides west with forty men, intending to summon Gisli to the Thing at Thorsness, and Thorkell, whey-Thorbjorn's son, goes with him, and Bork's nephews Thorodd and Saka-Stein; there was also a Norwegian in the party called Thorgrim.

They ride to Sandaoss. Then Thorkell spoke: 'I have a debt to collect at a small farm near here'—and he named the farm—'and I shall ride there and collect the debt while you come after me at your own pace.' He goes ahead; and when he got to the place he had spoken of, he asks the housewife to change horses with him and let his stand by the door—'and throw some home-spun over the saddle, and when my friends come along, tell them that I am sitting in the living-room and counting money'. She gives him another horse and he rides quickly and comes into the woods and meets Gisli and tells him what is going on, that Bork has come from the west.

20

GISLI ASKS HIS brother what he thinks is best to do, and he wants to know what Thorkell will do to help him, and whether he will give him shelter. He answers as before, that he will give him warning if any attacks are to be made, but he will keep himself clear of a law-case. Thorkell then rides off and takes a way that brings him up behind Bork and the others, and slows down their pace somewhat.

Gisli then hitches up two oxen and drives a cart with his valuables in it to the woods, and with him goes his thrall, Thord, the faint-hearted one. Then Gisli spoke: 'You have often been obedient to me, and done as I have asked you, and I ought to give you some good reward.'

It was Gisli's way to be well dressed, and in a blue cape; he takes the cape from his back then and said: 'I will give you this cape, friend, and I want you to have the good of it at once and put it on, and sit in the sledge behind, and I will lead the oxen and be dressed in your cloak.'

They do as he says. Then Gisli spoke. 'If it happens that anyone calls out to you, then you must be sure not to answer at all; and if anybody wants to hurt you, then you run to the woods.'

This fellow had as much sense as he had spirit, for he had none of either. Gisli now leads the oxen. Thord was a man of big build, and he sat high in the sledge; also he plumed himself rather, and thought himself splendidly dressed.

Now Bork and his company see them as they go towards the woods, and ride after them fast. And when Thord sees this he jumps off the sledge and runs as hard as he can to the trees. They think it is Gisli and ride their fastest after him, and shout at him loudly. But he keeps quiet and runs his hardest. Thorgrim the Norwegian throws a spear after him, and it hits him between the shoulders so hard that it throws him forward, and this was his death-wound.

Then Bork speaks: 'Well shot! It couldn't have been better!'

The brothers say that they will go after the thrall and see if there is any fight in him; so they go into the woods. The next thing is that Bork and the others come up to the blue-caped man and pull back his hood, and now it seems that their luck is less than they had thought, for they find Thord the faint-hearted where they had expected to find Gisli. And the story says now that the brothers come among the trees where Gisli is, and he sees them and they him. One of them throws his spear at him, and Gisli catches it in flight and throws it back at Thorodd, and it hits him in the middle and goes right through him. Stein turns back to his fellows and says the going is rather heavy in the woods. Bork, however, wants to carry on the chase, and so they do. And when they are among the trees Thorgrim the Norwegian sees where the branches move in a certain place, and he throws a spear there which hits Gisli in the calf of the leg. Gisli throws the spear back and it goes through Thorgrim, and he is killed.

They search the woods but they do not find Gisli, and they turn back then, leaving things as they are, to Gisli's house, and there they speak the summons against him for the slaying of Thorgrim. They get nothing from the house in the way of plunder, and ride home. Gisli goes up the mountainside behind the farm and binds up his wound while Bork and the others are at the steading. When they were gone Gisli went back to his house and got ready to move.

When Bork first got the case ready against him for hearing at the Thorsness Thing, Gisli sold his land to Thorkell Eiriksson and took payment in cash; this was much easier for him to handle. He takes a boat now, and puts his valuables in it, which were worth a large sum, and takes his wife Aud with him and his foster-daughter Gudrid, and goes out to Husaness and comes ashore there. Gisli goes up to the house there and meets a man, and the man asks him who he is, and Gisli told him what he thought fit, but not the whole truth. Gisli takes up a stone and throws it out to an island, which lay off shore there, and told the farmer to have his son do the same when he came home, and said that he would know then what man had come his way. For this was what no other man could do, and it showed, once more, that Gisli was better at such feats than most other men.

Gisli goes to his boat and rows out around the headland and across Arnarfjord and up into the fjord that runs in from Arnarfjord, which is called Geirthjofsfjord, and there he settles down, and he builds a full steading and stays there for the winter.

21

THE NEXT THING that happens is that Gisli sends word to Aud's kinsmen, Helgi and Sigurd and Vestgeir, asking them to go to the Thing and offer to pay a settlement for him so that he should not be outlawed. So these sons of Bjartmar go to the Thing, but they bring about no kind of settlement, and men say that they behaved badly and they were almost in tears before it was over. They tell Thorkell the rich what has happened, and said that they did not dare tell Gisli that he had been outlawed. Nothing else of note happened at the Thing besides Gisli's sentence.

Thorkell the rich goes to Gisli and told him that he had been outlawed. Then Gisli spoke this verse:

> ' They would not
> At Thorsness
> Have quailed thus
> In my case
> If Bjartmar's
> Sons' breasts
> Had harboured
> Vestein's heart.

> *Glum they were*
> *Who should be glad,*
> *Brothers of my*
> *Wife's mother:*
> *These gold-spenders*
> *Desponded*
> *As though sprayed*
> *By a bad egg.*
>
> *Word has come from northward*
> *To warn me, from Thorsness;*
> *Thing-men, unthewed, wronged me,*
> *Thorkell, in the court there.*
> *Bork and Stein will brook my*
> *Bitter coin, in witness,*
> *Well earned, of my ill will,*
> *Weighed and fully paid them.'*

Gisli asks the two Thorkells what he can expect of them. They tell him that they will give him shelter, as long as they do not lose their property on account of it. Then they ride home.

It is told that Gisli was three years in Geirthjofsfjord, but now and again with Thorkell Eiriksson, and the next three years he goes all about Iceland and visits the chieftains and asks for their help, but because of the black power that Thorgrim neb had put into his spell-casting and cursing, he did not succeed in getting a chieftain to take up with him, and although sometimes they seemed not unlikely to favour him, something always got in the way. He stayed for long stretches, however, with Thorkell Eiriksson, and he has now been an outlaw for six years.

After this he stays sometimes with Aud in the house in Geirthjofsfjord, and sometimes in a hiding-place north of the river which he had made for himself; he had another hiding-place by the cliffs south of the river, and sometimes he stayed there.

22

NOW WHEN BORK hears of all this he makes a trip to see Eyjolf the grey, who lived then in Otradal on Arnarfjord, and asks him to hunt for Gisli and kill him as an outlaw, and he says that he will give him sixty ounces of the purest silver if he will make every effort to hunt for him. Eyjolf takes the money and agrees to carry out the hunt.

A man was with Eyjolf whose name was Helgi, and he was called spying Helgi: he was both quick on his feet and sharp-sighted, and he knew all the country round the fjords. He is sent into Geirthjofsfjord to find out whether Gisli is there. He sees that there is a man, but does not know whether it is Gisli or someone else. He goes home and tells Eyjolf what he has found. Eyjolf says he is sure it must have been Gisli, and he acts quickly and goes off with six men into Geirthjofsfjord, but he sees no sign of Gisli, so he comes back home, having done nothing.

Gisli was a wise man, and one who dreamed dreams that had true meanings. It is agreed among all wise men that Gisli went longer as an outlaw than any other man, except Grettir Asmundsson. The story says that one autumn Gisli had a struggle in his sleep one night, when he was staying at Aud's steading; and when he awoke, she asked him what he had been dreaming.

He answers. 'I have two women in my dreams,' he says, 'and one is good to me, but the other always tells me something that makes me feel worse than before, and she foresees nothing but bad for me. And this time in my dream I seemed to come to a house, or a hall, and I seemed to go into the house, and there I recognized many of those who were inside, kinsmen of mine, and friends. They were sitting by the fires and drinking, and there were seven fires—some were nearly burnt out, and some were burning very brightly. Then came in my better dream woman and said that these marked my life, what I had yet to live; and she counselled me that while I lived I should give up the old faith, and have nothing to do with magic or witchcraft, and deal kindly with the blind and the halt and the poor and the helpless. There was no more to the dream.' Then Gisli spoke some verses:

> ' Wife, land of the wave fire,
> Where I came were flaming
> Seven fires to my sorrow,
> Stern, in the hall burning;
> Bench crews rose and bowed there
> From board seats to greet me;
> In return I answered
> Old meet words of greeting.

Bend your eyes, band goddess
Bade me, glad spender,
Fires, your life foretelling,
Furnish the hall, burning.
Years are few of yearning
Yet, until a better
Time for you, storm tamer,
Treader of sword weather.

Let your heart from learning
Lightness, and in right wise,
Schooled by good scalds, said she,
Seek the best, unresting.
Worst lot for the waster
Of wave fire, brave spender,
Ever, to know evil
Is, men say, in wisdom.

Hold your blade from bloodshed,
Be not first to stir them
Nor press them, promise me,
The proud gods of slaughter.
Help the blind and handless,
And heed this, ring-speeder,
Low the mocker's fame lies
And lame-harmer's name, low.'

23

NOW IS TO BE told how Bork keeps egging on Eyjolf, and thinks
the business not as well followed up as he would like it to be, and
thinks that he has not got much for the money he has paid over,
and he says that he knows for certain that Gisli is in Geirthjofsfjord, and he tells Eyjolf's men that have been sent between the
two of them that Eyjolf must hunt for Gisli or else, he says, he
will go after him himself. Eyjolf then bestirs himself and again
sends spying Helgi into Geirthjofsfjord, and this time he has food
with him and is away for a week, and he keeps watch for a sight

34

of Gisli. He sees him one day when he is going from his hiding-place, and recognizes him; this is what he has been waiting for, and he goes back and tells Eyjolf what he has found out. Eyjolf gets ready and sets out for Geirthjofsfjord with eight men, and goes to Aud's farmhouse; they do not find Gisli there, and they range the woods all round, hunting for him, and do not find him; they come back then to Aud's house and Eyjolf offers her much money to tell them where Gisli is, but it is far from her mind to do that. Then they threaten to hurt her, but this has no effect, and they must go home empty-handed.

People thought this trip could not have been more con-temptible, and Eyjolf stays at home for the rest of the fall. Although Gisli was not found this time, he reasons that he is, nevertheless, bound to be taken, when he is such a short distance from Eyjolf's farm. Gisli leaves home now, and rides out to Bardastrand and comes to see his brother Thorkell at Hvamm. He knocks at the door of the sleeping-quarters where Thorkell is, and Thorkell comes out and greets him.

'Now I want to know,' said Gisli, 'if you will give me some help; I expect good help from you, because I am hard pressed, and I have held off asking you for a long while.'

Thorkell answers as before and says that he will give him no help which might bring a case against him, and says that he will give him money, or a horse if he needed one, or anything else like this, as he had said before.

'I see now,' said Gisli, 'that you will give me no real help. Give me three hundred and sixty ells of homespun, and comfort your-self with the thought that I will not often trouble you for help again.'

Thorkell does so, gives him cloth, and some silver as well. Gisli says that he will accept that too, and went on to say that he would not treat him so meanly, however, if he stood in his place. Gisli is moved when they part. He goes now to Vadil, to Gest Oddleifsson's mother, and comes there before daylight and knocks. She answers the door. It was often her way to take in outlaws, and she had an underground room; one way into the underground room was by the river, and the other was in her kitchen, and traces of it can still be seen.

Thorgerd welcomes Gisli—'and I will let you stay here for a while, but I do not know whether I can give you anything but a woman's help here'. Gisli says that he will accept, and says that men's help had not been so good that it would be unlikely that women's help would not be better. Gisli is there over the winter, and nowhere was he better treated during his outlawry.

24

As soon as it is spring Gisli goes back to Geirthjofsfjord, and he cannot be away from his wife Aud any longer, so devoted are they to one another; he is hidden there over the summer and until fall. And then the dreams come on again, as soon as the nights grow long; and the worse dream woman comes to him now, and he has hard dreams, and once he tells Aud what he has dreamed when she asked him, and then he spoke a verse:

> '*If dreams true lines draw me*
> *Dark for age they mark me;*
> *Thread-work goddess through my*
> *Thought-filled sleep has sought me.*
> *Although the ale goddess*
> *Invites no bright meaning,*
> *Linker of strong letters*
> *Not less soundly rests him.*'

Then Gisli says that the worse woman comes to him often, and is always wanting to smear him with gore and blood, and wash him in it, and she carries on hideously. Then he spoke another verse:

> '*Not every dream avails me,*
> *Albeit word not fails me;*
> *She, goddess, has spoken,*
> *So is my joy broken.*
> *At sleep's edge she seeks me,*
> *With slaughter's gilt freaks me;*
> *This woman works bloody*
> *Wound flood on me, ruddy.*'

And again he spoke:

> '*Told have I the tall ones,*
> *Trees of the spear's greeting,*
> *My dream of death's coming,*
> *Dear wealth goddess, clearly.*

Seekers of sark's hatred,
Strife gods, who outlawed me,
Will feel my filed weapon's
Fang, if I grow angry.'

And now things are quiet. Gisli goes to Thorgerd and stays another winter with her. The following summer he goes to Geirthjofsfjord and is there until the fall. Then he goes again to his brother Thorkell's place and knocks on the door. Thorkell will not come out, so Gisli takes up a stick and cuts runes on it and throws it in. Thorkell sees it and picks it up and looks at it, and then stands up and goes out and greets Gisli and asks for his news. He says that he has none to tell him—'And I have come to see you for the last time, brother, and let your help now be worthier; and I shall pay you by never asking help from you again'.

Thorkell replies again the same as before—he offers him a horse or a boat but refuses to stand by him himself. Gisli accepts the boat and asks Thorkell to help him launch it. He does so— and brings him four hundred and eighty pounds of food and a hundred and twenty ells of homespun. And when Gisli has got into the boat, Thorkell stands on the shore.

Then Gisli spoke. 'Now you think that you are in clover, and the friend of many chieftains, and you have nothing to fear; and I am an outlaw, and many men are my bitter enemies; but I can tell you this, that you will be killed before me. We must now part, and on worse terms than ought to be, and we shall never see each other again; and you must know that I would never deal with you like this.'

'I am not worried by your prophecies,' said Thorkell, and they part like this.

Gisli rows out to the island Hergilsey in Breidafjord. He takes out of the boat the decking and thwarts and oars and everything not fixed in, and he overturns the boat and lets it wash ashore in the Nesses. And men guess, when they see the boat, that Gisli has been drowned, since the boat is wrecked and washed up, and that he must have taken it from his brother Thorkell.

Now Gisli goes up on Hergilsey, to the house. A man lives there whose name was Ingjald; his wife's name was Thorgerd; Ingjald was Gisli's cousin, and had come out to Iceland with him. When they meet he offers Gisli shelter and any help he can give him; and Gisli accepts and stays there in quiet for a while.

25

THERE WAS A thrall with Ingjald, and a bondwoman; the thrall was named Svart and the bondwoman was named Bothild. Helgi was the name of Ingjald's son, and he was as simple as could be, and a fool; a tether was made for him, a stone with a hole in it was tied to his neck and he browsed the grass out of doors like the cattle, and he was called Ingjald's fool. He was a big man, almost a giant.

Gisli is there over the winter, and he builds a boat for Ingjald, and many other things. And whatever he made was easy to recognize because he was handier than most other men. Men began to wonder why so many things were well made that Ingjald had; for he was not good with his hands. Gisli is always in Geirthjofs-fjord over the summer; three years have now passed from the time he had begun to dream, and this is the best shelter he has had, which Ingjald gives him.

It seems to men, now, that all these things taken together are suspicious, and they begin to think that Gisli must be alive, and that he must have been living with Ingjald and not drowned, as had been said. Men begin to talk about the fact that Ingjald now has three boats, and all well made. These rumours come to the ears of Eyjolf the grey, and it falls to Helgi's lot to set out again, and he comes to Hergilsey.

Gisli is always in an underground room when anyone comes to the island. But Ingjald was a hospitable man, and he offers Helgi a bed; so he was there for the night. Ingjald was a hard-working man; he rowed out to fish every day that the weather was fit; and in the morning, when he was ready to set out, he asks whether Helgi is not keen to get on with his journey, and why is he still in bed? He said that he was not quite well, and he breathed heavily and rubbed his head. Ingjald told him to lie still then, and he rows out to sea; and Helgi takes to groaning hard. Now the story says that Thorgerd goes to the underground room and means to give Gisli his breakfast; and there is a partition between the pantry and the room Helgi was lying in; Thorgerd goes out of the pantry; Helgi climbs up on the partition and sees that somebody's food has been set out; and at this Thorgerd comes back in, and Helgi moves fast, and he falls down from the partition. Thorgerd asks why he is doing this, climbing up in the rafters, and not lying still. He says that he is so frantic with the pains in his limbs that he cannot lie still—'and I wish,' he says, 'that you would help me back to bed'. She does so. Then she goes out with the food. But Helgi gets straight out of bed and follows her, and sees now what is going on; he goes back and lies down after this and stays there for the day.

Ingjald comes home in the evening and goes to Helgi's bed and asks whether he is any better. He says he has taken a turn for the better, and he asks to be ferried off the island in the morning; so he is taken south to Flatey, and from there he makes his way to Thorsness; and he tells them that he has found out that Gisli is with Ingjald. Bork sets out then by ship with fourteen men, and sails north across Breidafjord. This day Ingjald has rowed out to fish and Gisli with him, and the thrall and the bondwoman in another boat, and they were lying off some islands that are called Skutileyjar.

26

Now INGJALD SEES the ship sailing from the south, and he said: 'A ship is sailing there, and I think it will be Bork the stout.'

'What should we do now?' asked Gisli. 'I want to find out if you are a clever man, as much as you are a stout fellow.'

'I can decide quickly,' said Ingjald, 'though I may not be clever; let us row as hard as we can to the island and then climb up on Vadsteinaberg and fight, as long as we can stand.'

'That is what I expected,' said Gisli, 'that you would offer a plan that calls for the best courage; but I make a worse payment for your help than I intended if you lose your life for my sake. That must never be, and we shall follow another plan. You shall row to the island with the thrall and go up on the hill and make a stand to defend yourselves, and they will think I am the other man with you when they sail north around the headland. And I shall change clothes with the thrall, as I have done once before now, and I shall go in the boat with Bothild.'

Ingjald did as Gisli advised; and one thing was apparent, that he was very angry. And as the boats separate the bondwoman spoke: 'What is to be done now?' Gisli answered in a verse:

'*Woman, this wight, deeming*
His wing turned from Ingjald,
Plans, and plies his cunning
—I pour the dwarfs' liquor.
Whether ill or well fare
Awaits me, I mate it
Boldly, splendid bond-wife,
Bright tree of the sea's fire.'

Now they row south towards Bork and his men and look as
though they expected no trouble. Then Gisli tells her what he
wants her to do. 'You shall say,' he says, 'that this is the fool in
the boat; and I shall sit in the bows and mimic him, and tangle
myself in the lines and hang overboard sometimes and carry on
as foolishly as I know how; and if we get past them a little, I shall
row my hardest and try to put distance between us as fast as
possible.'

She rows on towards them and yet not too close, and makes it
look as though she is going to another fishing ground. Bork calls
out to her and asks if Gisli is on the island.

'I do not know that,' says she, 'but I do know that there is a
man there who is both bigger than other men, those who are on
the island, and better with his hands.'

'Ay,' says Bork. 'And is farmer Ingjald at home?'

'A while ago he rowed to the island,' said she, 'and his thrall
with him, or so I thought.'

'That will not have been a thrall,' says Bork; 'that must have
been Gisli—and let us row after them as fast as we can.'

His men kept their eyes on Gisli and answered: 'We think
there is some sport here with the half-wit: look at the fool things
he is doing!' They told Bothild that she was badly off, having to
look after this idiot.

'I think so too,' she says. 'But it's my belief you are making a
joke of it, and do not feel sorry for me at all.'

'No more of this foolishness,' says Bork. 'Let us get on our
way.'

They leave her and row to the island and go ashore, and then
they see the men up on Vadsteinaberg, and they go up after them,
and think that everything is going their way; for Ingjald and his
thrall have taken their stand on the crag. Bork knows the men
right away, and he spoke to Ingjald: 'You will be wise to give up
Gisli, or else tell me where he is; and you are a son of a bitch to

shelter my brother's murderer when you are my tenant, and it's bad treatment you deserve from me, and it would only be right if you were killed.'

Ingjald answers: 'My clothes are threadbare, and it will not grieve me not to make them more so; and I will rather lose my life than not do Gisli any good turn that I can, or keep him from trouble.'

And men have said that Ingjald gave Gisli most help, and that his help was the most useful to him; and the story says that when Thorgrim neb worked his curse he spoke in this way, that Gisli should get no benefit even though men should help him here on the mainland; but it did not come into his head to say anything that covered the off-shore islands, and so this help lasted rather longer than any other, though it was bound to come to an end.

27

BORK DOES NOT think it proper to attack Ingjald, his tenant; they go away then to the house and hunt for Gisli there, and do not find him, as was to be expected. They go about the island and come to the place where the fool was, browsing grass in a little dale with a stone tied around his neck. Then Bork has something to say. 'Not only is Ingjald's fool much spoken of, but he is in rather more places than I thought, and it is no good staring at him here. We have been so careless that it is hard to believe; and I can hardly see how we shall put it right again. That will have been Gisli in the boat near us, making out that he was the idiot; because he has the wit for anything and he is a great mimic; but it will be most shameful if he slips through our fingers, so many of us as we are; we must go quick after him and not let him get out of range.'

Then they jump into their ship and row after them, and pull fast on the oars. Soon they see that Gisli and the bondwoman have gone far into the sound, and now both boats row hard. The larger boat, with the more men in it, goes faster, and comes up so near at last that Bork is within spear-shot of him, but by then Gisli has come to shore. Then Gisli speaks, and said to the bond-woman: 'We shall part now, and here is a gold ring that you shall take to Ingjald, and another for his wife, and tell them that they are to give you your freedom, and take these as tokens. I also want Svart to be given his freedom. You must surely be called the one who has saved my life, and I want you to be rewarded for it.'

They part, and Gisli climbs ashore and up to a rocky cleft; he was on an islet on the coast of Hjardarness. The bondwoman rowed away, sweating from the exertion, and reeking of it.

The ship comes to shore and Saka-Stein is the first out of it, and he climbs up to look for Gisli; and when he reaches the cleft Gisli is standing there with his drawn sword, and he brings it right down on his head so that it splits him to the shoulder, and he fell dead to the ground. Bork and the rest now go up on the island; but Gisli jumps down into the sea, intending to swim to the mainland. Bork throws a spear after him, which takes him in the leg and cuts right through, and it makes a bad wound. He pulls the spear out, but he loses his sword because he was so weary that he could not keep his grip on it. It was dark by then. When he reached the shore he goes into the woods, for there was much bush land there then. Bork and the others row over to the mainland and hunt for Gisli, and they surround him in the woods, and he is so tired and stiff that he can hardly walk, and he is aware of men all around him. He tries to think of a way out, and he comes down to the water's edge and makes his way round to Haug in the darkness along the foreshore which was passable on the ebb, and he meets a certain farmer called Ref.

This farmer was a very cunning man. He greets Gisli and asks him for his news. He told him everything that had happened between him and Bork. Ref had a wife called Alfdis, handsome in looks but violent in temper, and altogether a shrew; she was a match for Ref. When he has told Ref his news, Gisli asks him for help—'for they will be here soon,' said Gisli, 'and they are pressing me hard, and there are not many I can turn to for help.'

'I shall make one condition,' said Ref, 'that however I go about helping you, you will not interfere at all.'

'I agree to that,' said Gisli, 'and I shall not walk a step farther.'

'Go inside, then,' said Ref; and so they did.

Then Ref spoke to Alfdis: 'Now I am going to change men in bed with you,'—and he takes all the covers off the bed, and said that Gisli was to lie down there in the straw, and he puts the covers back over him, and Alfdis gets back in bed on top of him

—'and you stay there,' said Ref, 'for the time being, whatever happens.' He tells Alfdis now to be on her worst behaviour, and as though she was out of her mind—'and do not hold back,' said Ref. 'Say whatever bad thing comes into your head, curses and bad language; and I will go and do the talking with them, and pick my words to suit myself.'

And for the second time, when he comes out, he sees men approaching, and these are Bork's companions, eight of them together. Bork is behind, at Forsa. These men had been sent up there to hunt for Gisli and take him if he has come this way. Ref is outside, and he asks for their news.

'We can only tell you what you must have heard already. But do you know anything about where Gisli has gone?' they ask. 'Has he perhaps come here?'

'I will give you two answers,' said Ref. 'He has not come here, and if he had tried it he would have met with swift disaster; and I do not know whether you think it is true or not that I am as ready as any one of you to kill Gisli; but I have enough wit to think that it would be no small gain to have the confidence of such a man as Bork is, and I want to be his friend.'

They ask: 'Will you mind if we search you and your home?'

'By all means,' says Ref. 'I shall be very glad of it, because I know that then you can search more surely in other places, if you know for certain first that he is not here; so go in and search the place inside out.'

They go in. And when Alfdis heard their noise she asks what thugs were on the move out there, or what kind of hooligans they were, bothering people in the night. Ref told her to quiet down. But she lets go a flood of bad language; she tells them a few things that they will not quickly forget. They carry out their search all the same, but not as thoroughly as they would have done if they had not first had to put up with such bad language from the housewife. They go away then, having found nothing, and wish the farmer a good life; and he wishes them good travelling. Then they come back to Bork—and they are all dissatisfied with this trip, and they think that they have had a great and shameful loss in Saka-Stein, without achieving anything they had set out for. The news goes about the district, and nobody can see any difference between this and their other failures against Gisli. Bork goes home now, and tells Eyjolf how things stand.

Gisli stays with Ref for a fortnight, then he goes away, and parts good friends with Ref, and gives him a knife and belt, which were valuable things; they were all he had left on him. Afterwards he goes back to his wife in Geirthjofsfjord, and he has added a great deal to his fame by this adventure. And it is true to say that there has not been such a powerful man as Gisli, nor one so courageous, and yet he was not lucky. But it is time to speak of something else.

28

IT IS TO BE told now that in the spring Bork goes to the Thing in Thorskafjord with a large party of men, with the purpose of meeting his friends. Gest comes from the west, from Raudasand on Bardastrand, and also Thorkell, the son of whey-Thorbjorn, each sailing his own ship. And when Gest is ready to set out, two boys come to him, badly dressed and carrying staves in their hands. It becomes known for certain that Gest has a talk in private with the boys, and it is also certain that they ask for passage on his ship and he gives it to them. They go as far as Hallsteinsness with him, and there he puts them ashore east of the farm on the headland called Grenitresness. From here they make their own way to the assembly.

There was a man named Hallbjorn; he was a tramp who used to go about the country, never with fewer men than ten or twelve; and he had built himself a booth at the Thing. The boys go there and ask for shelter in his booth, and say they are tramps. He says he will give booth-room to anyone who will ask him for it.

'I have been here many springs,' he said, 'and I know all the noblemen and chiefs.'

The boys say that they will be glad of his protection, and want to learn from him—'we are very curious to see the famous men that the big stories are about'. Hallbjorn says that he will go down to the shore, and he said that he would recognize every ship as soon as it came in, and tell them. They thank him for being so friendly. Then they go down to the shore and across to the water's edge; and they see that some ships are sailing in. The older boy speaks. 'Whose is that ship, that is sailing this way first?'

Hallbjorn said that it was Bork the stout's ship.

'And who is sailing next to him?'

'Gest the wise,' he said.

44

'And who is sailing after him, and drawing up there in the creek mouth?'

'That is Thorkell, son of whey-Thorbjorn,' he said.

They see now that Thorkell goes ashore and sits down on the ground, while their gear is being carried off to a point above high-water mark. And Bork gets their booth ready. Thorkell had a Russian fur hat on his head, and a grey cloak fastened with a gold pin at the shoulder, and a sword in his hand. Then Hallbjorn goes over, and the two boys with him, to where Thorkell is sitting. Now one of the boys, the older one, speaks:

'Who is this lordly man sitting here? I have not seen such a handsome and noble-looking man.'

'Your words are well spoken; and I am called Thorkell.'

The boy says: 'That must be a valuable sword that you have in your hand; will you let me have a look at it?'

Thorkell answers: 'It is a very strange thing you ask, but I will let you see it.' And he hands it to him.

The boy took the sword and turned aside a little, and undoes the peace-straps and draws the sword from the scabbard.

When Thorkell saw this, he said: 'I did not give you leave to draw the sword.'

'I did not ask your leave,' said the boy, and he swings the sword back and drives it into Thorkell's neck so that the blow took off his head.

As soon as this has happened Hallbjorn the tramp jumps up; the boy throws the bloody sword down, and picks up his staff, and the two of them run with Hallbjorn and his gang; and the tramps are nearly off their heads with panic. They run up by the booth which Bork is getting ready. Men crowd around Thorkell, and nobody seems to know who has done the deed.

Bork asks what this excitement and noise means that is going on around Thorkell. And when Hallbjorn and his gang run up by the booth—there were fifteen tramps—and when Bork asks this question, the younger boy answers him, whose name was Helgi— the one who had done the killing was called Berg—'I do not know what they are meeting about; but I think they are trying to decide whether Vestein left only daughters or had sons too.'

Hallbjorn runs to his booth; and the boys go into the scrub that was round about and are not found again.

29

MEN COME RUNNING now to Hallbjorn's booth and ask what it all means. The tramps say that two young boys had come into their gang, and they say they had no inkling of this, and they say that they knew nothing at all about them; they tell something, however, about their looks, and what sort of things they had said. Bork thinks he knows now from the words Helgi had spoken that it must have been the sons of Vestein; and so he goes to see Gest and talk over with him how he should go about this business.

Bork says: 'It is more my duty than anyone else's to take up Thorkell's case, since he was my brother-in-law. It seems not unlikely to us that this is how it happened, that Vestein's sons must have done the deed; because we do not know that any other man would be likely to have anything against Thorkell, except them. It may be that they have got away for now. Tell me what you think: how should the case be taken up?'

Gest answers, 'I would know what to do if I had done the killing; I would use the trick—so that the case would fail that might be brought against me—of calling myself by another name', and Gest puts many difficulties in the way of bringing a case forward. People have been sure that Gest was in the plot with the boys, because he was tied to them by kinship.

They break off their talk, and the case is dropped. And Thorkell is buried with the old rites, and men go home from the Thing; and nothing else of importance happens at this assembly. Bork was discontented with his trip, as he had often had cause to be, and he had furthermore brought on himself much disgrace and dishonour from this affair, the way things had been left.

The boys go on until they come to Geirthjofsfjord, spending five days and nights in the open country. Then they come to Aud's steading, and Gisli is there at the time; they come at night and knock on the door. Aud opens it and greets them and asks for their news. Gisli was in the bed-closet beneath which there was an underground passage, and she would raise her voice if he needed to be on guard. They tell her about the killing of Thorkell and about how they are managing; and they tell her also how long they have been without food.

'I am going to send you,' said Aud, 'across the ridge to

Mosdal, to Bjartmar's sons; I shall give you food and a token so that they will give you shelter; and I am doing this because I do not want to ask Gisli to help you.'

The boys go into the woods, where they might not be found, and eat the food, for they had gone hungry for a long time; and then they lie down to sleep when they had eaten their fill, because they were very tired.

30

NOW IT IS TO be said of Aud that she goes in to Gisli and spoke: 'It means much to me now how you will take this, so as to treat me more honourably than I deserve.'

He understood her at once and said: 'I know that you are going to tell me of the killing of my brother Thorkell.'

'It is as you have guessed,' said Aud, 'and the boys came here and they wanted to hide out with you, and they thought they could put their trust in nothing but this.'

He answers: 'I cannot bear to see my brother's killers, and be together with them,' and he jumps up and goes to draw his sword, and he spoke a verse:

> '*Guess not but that Gisli,*
> *Given this cause, driven*
> *By thought of slain Thorkell,*
> *—Thing tidings men bring him—*
> *Battle ice but that he*
> *Brandish may in answer.*
> *Doubt not. I will dare till*
> *Death has made me breathless.*'

Then Aud said that they were gone—'for I had wit enough not to risk them here'.

Gisli said that this was the best way, that they should not meet; and he becomes calmer at once, and things are then quiet for a while. It is said that now there are no more than two years left of those that the dream woman said he would live. And as the season wears on Gisli stays in Geirthjofsfjord, and the dreams all return and the hard struggles in his sleep, and now it is always the worse dream woman who comes to him, except for odd times when it is the better. One night it happens that the better dream

47

woman again comes to him; she seemed to be riding a grey
horse, and she invites him to ride with her to her home, and he
goes with her. They come now to a house which is very like a
nobleman's hall, and she leads him into it by the hand, and it
seems to him that there are cushions along the raised benches,
and all the furnishings are rich. She asked that they should stay
there together and be happy—'and you shall come here when you
die,' she said, 'and enjoy riches and contentment'. Then he
wakes up, and he spoke some verses about what he had dreamt:

> *'Goddess of threads gladly*
> *On her grey steed prayed me*
> *Rise up, praise-rune maker,*
> *Ride away beside her.*
> *Golden one, of seagull's*
> *Ground, in weakness found me;*
> *To help me and heal me*
> *Her grave promise gave me.*
>
> *Splendid sea-flame goddess*
> *Showed me, ode-contriver,*
> *Where, for my worn body*
> *And will, lay a pillow.*
> *Linen goddess led me*
> *Lo, where sleep would know me;*
> *No hilled pallet held me;*
> *My head, sweetly bedded.*
>
> *Hither, when death's heavy*
> *Handblow has unmanned you,*
> *Said then that sweet lady,*
> *Shall the valkyr bring you.*
> *Adder's earth and other*
> *Old rich treasure told here*
> *And my self you solely*
> *Sovereign shall govern.'*

3 1

THEN THE STORY says that a time comes when Helgi was again
sent spying into Geirthjofsfjord; and people think it likely that

Gisli is there. A man goes with him whose name is Havard. He had come to Iceland that summer, and he was a kinsman of Gest Oddleifsson. They were sent into the woods to cut timber, and so they made their business appear to be, but in fact they were meant to look for Gisli and see if they could find his hiding-place. And one day at twilight they see a fire in the cliffs to the south of the river. This was at nightfall, when it was already quite dark. Havard asks Helgi what they should do about this—'for you,' he says, 'will be more used to this business than I'.

'There is one thing to do,' says Helgi. 'Build a cairn here on this hillock where we are standing, so that we can find it again when it is daylight; and we can take a sight across from the cairn to the cliffs, which are not far to see.'

They follow this plan. When they have built the cairn, Havard said that he was sleepy, so much so that he could no longer stay awake. He lies down and sleeps. But Helgi stays awake and does what is needed to finish the cairn. When he has done this, Havard wakes up and tells Helgi to sleep, and he says that he will watch. So Helgi sleeps for a while. And while he is sleeping Havard goes to work and takes the cairn all apart and scatters the stones in the darkness. And when he has done all this he takes a big stone and smashes it down on the rock-face near Helgi's head, so that the earth shook with it. Helgi springs up, and he is shaking and frightened, and he asked what was happening.

Havard said: 'There is a man in the woods, and many stones like this have been coming down tonight.'

'It must have been Gisli,' says Helgi, 'and he must have found out that we are here; and you realize, man dear,' he says, 'that we will be smashed if such a stone hits us; and there is nothing else to do but get away as quickly as we can.'

Helgi runs off at his fastest; and Havard walks after him and asks Helgi not to leave him like that; but Helgi paid no attention and went as fast as his feet would go. At last they both come to their boat and jump into it and plunge the oars into the water and row hard, without letting up, until they come home to Otradal, and Helgi says he is sure now where Gisli is.

Eyjolf acts at once, and sets out with eleven men, and Helgi and Havard are in the party. They go on into Geirthjofsfjord and range through all the woods, hunting for the cairn and Gisli's hiding-place, but they found neither. Then Eyjolf asks Havard where they had built the cairn.

He answers: 'I cannot be sure of that; because not only was I so tired that I hardly knew what was going on around me, but besides Helgi finished building the cairn while I was sleeping. I think it is not unlikely that Gisli knew we were there, and he carried away the cairn when it was daylight, and we had left.'

Eyjolf said: 'We have had nothing but bad luck in this case, and we may as well turn back,' and so they do, but Eyjolf says he will visit Aud first. They come to the steading and walk in, and Eyjolf settled down again to have a talk with Aud. He has this to say: 'I will make a bargain with you, Aud,' he says, 'that you tell me where Gisli is and I will give you the sixty ounces of silver which I have taken as the price on his head. You shall not be there when we take his life. It will also follow that I will arrange a marriage for you that will be better in every way than this one has been. You can see for yourself,' he says, 'how miserable it becomes for you, living in this deserted fjord, and having this happen to you because of Gisli's bad luck, and never seeing your kinsfolk or their families.'

She answers: 'I think the last thing,' she says, 'that we are likely to agree about is that you could arrange any marriage for me that I would think as good as this one. Even so, it is true, as they say, that "cash is the widow's best comfort"; and let me see whether this silver is as much or as fine as you say it is.'

He pours the silver into her lap then, and she puts her hand into it while he counts it and turns it over before her. Gudrid, her foster-daughter, begins to cry.

32

SHE GOES OUT and finds Gisli, and she says to him: 'My foster-mother has gone out of her wits, and she is going to betray you.'

Gisli spoke. 'Put your mind at rest, for it will not be treachery from Aud that will be the cause of my death.' And he spoke a verse:

> *'Loud they tongue my lady,*
> *Lords of masted fjord-elks;*
> *Hoards she, say they, hard thoughts*
> *Heart deep for her partner.*

I have seen that single
Sorrow keeps she, mourning;
True drops, never traitor
Tears fall from my dear one.'

Then the girl goes home again and says nothing of where she has been. Eyjolf has then counted the silver, and Aud spoke: 'In no way is the silver less or poorer than you have said; and you will think now that I have the right to do with it as I please.'

Eyjolf agrees with this gladly, and tells her certainly to do what she likes with it.

Aud takes the silver and puts it in a big purse; she stands up and swings the purse with the silver in it at Eyjolf's nose, so that the blood spurts out all over him; then she spoke: 'Take that for your easy faith, and every harm with it! There was never any likelihood that I would give my husband over to you, scoundrel. Take your money, and shame and disgrace with it! You will remember, as long as you live, you miserable man, that a woman has struck you; and yet you will not get what you want for all that!'

Then Eyjolf said: 'Seize the bitch and kill her, woman or not!'

Havard has something to say: 'This errand has been poor enough, without this coward's work. Stand up, men, and do not let him get his way in this.'

Eyjolf said: 'The old saying is true: "A man's worst following comes from home".'

Havard was a well-liked man, and many of them were ready to back him up, besides wanting to turn Eyjolf from a bad act; and Eyjolf has to be satisfied to leave it at this and go.

Before Havard went out Aud spoke to him: 'It would be wrong not to pay you the debt that Gisli owes you, and here is a gold finger-ring that I want you to have.'

'I would not have claimed it,' says Havard.

'I want to pay it, though,' says Aud. She was really giving him the ring for the help he had given her.

Havard got himself a horse and rides south to Bardastrand, to Gest Oddleifsson, and he refuses to stay with Eyjolf any longer. Eyjolf goes home to Otradal, discontented with what had been done; and indeed it was everywhere thought to have been most contemptible.

33

AS THE SUMMER passes Gisli remains in his hiding-places, being
wary for himself, and he has made up his mind not to go away
again; it seems to him now that his burrows are all snowed in;
and the years allotted to him in his dreams are all spent. Then
comes a certain night in summer when Gisli has a bad sleep. And
when he wakens Aud asks him what he has dreamt. He says that
the worse dream woman came to him and spoke: 'Now I shall
overturn everything that the better woman has told you; and I
shall see to it that no good will come to you of anything she has
promised.' Then he spoke a verse:

> '*Sorrow will you sever,*
> *Such as deep love touches,*
> *Turn your ways in torment,*
> *Told me the bowl goddess.*
> *Lord of life has led you*
> *Lone, to unknown places,*
> *Hills far from your hall roof,*
> *Homeless, new world roamer.*'

'I dreamt further,' he said, 'that this woman came to me and
tied a bloody cap on my head, after she had washed my head in
blood, and she spattered me all over so that I was all bloody.'
He spoke a verse:

> '*I dreamt the dread goddess*
> *Drenched my head in redness,*
> *Froth of fires of Othin*
> *That flows where the blows fall.*
> *Goddess hands were hidden*
> *Of hawk-track fire, brackish*
> *Sword-loosed tides swept round them,*
> *Stained them deep with wound rain.*'

And again he spoke:

> '*I dreamt the doom goddess*
> *Draped my bushy straight-cut*
> *Hair with a dour head piece,*
> *Hat all blood bespattered;*

Seared with smoking sword rain
Her soiled hands embroiled me;
Thread-work goddess thrust me
Then to my dream's ending.'

Now the dreams become so much for Gisli, and he becomes so frightened of the dark that he is afraid to be alone; and as soon as his eyelids close the same woman appears to him. It was on one of these nights that Gisli struggled very hard in his sleep. Aud asked what had appeared to him.

'I dreamt,' says Gisli, 'that men were attacking us, and Eyjolf was among them, and many other men, and we met, and I knew that there was fighting between us. One of them came in front, bellowing loud, and I seemed to cut him in two at the middle, and I thought he had a wolf's head. Then more of them attacked me; I seemed to have a shield in my hand, and I kept them off for a long while.' Gisli spoke a verse:

'I fought a lone fateful
Fight, this was my nightmare;
Single, not soon was I
Slain by their main power.
Good flesh by my gashing
Gave I mouths of ravens,
But in your white bosom
Bright blood drops fell ruddy.'

And he spoke another:

'My shield fenced my scald's life,
The sounding blades found my
Wooden bastion wide-hard
Towards them, loud sword points.
Metal dinned on meeting;
Much their power touched me,
Quelled me, though my called-for
Courage faced their murder.'

And he spoke another:

'Ill fared one crow feeder
Before the rest tore me;
I carved for the curved-bill
Corpse-stream hawk this morsel;

Hewed strong legs my hard edge
Unhurried, struck surely;
Mastered, he missed footing,
More to swell my glory.'

The autumn was coming on and the dreams were not growing less but rather they came more often than before. It was one night when Gisli had again had a hard time in his sleep. Aud then asked him once more what had appeared to him. Gisli spoke a verse:

'My both sides were bathed in
Blood, I dreamed so, flooded;
I dreamed harm descended
Of drawn wound flood on me.
Necklet goddess, nightly
Now, blood nightmares bow me;
A storm stirs, of weapons,
Strife of men against me.'

He spoke another verse:

'It seemed gods of slain net
Set with blades whetted,
Blood on my both shoulders,
Broad and straight, ring goddess.
Ire of corpse-stream eagle's
Eye-delight providers
Left me dwindled life hopes,
Less to come of blessing.'

And again another:

'Sheared they with their sword blades—
Shield troll-woman wielders—
My doomed arms; I dreamt they
Deeply harmed my sleep self.
I dreamt the helm-daunting
Downward sword teeth gored me,
Greedy mouths, thread goddess,
Gaped at me their fang shapes.'

And he spoke still another verse:

> *'Band goddess bent to me,*
> *Bore for me dream sorrow,*
> *Fresh dew on her eye-fringe*
> *Felt that bright belt goddess.*
> *Soft that sea-fire goddess*
> *And soon, bound my wounds up:*
> *Ministered or meant she*
> *More, think you, than sorrow?'*

34

GISLI SPENDS THE whole summer at home, and all is quiet. Then comes the last day of the summer season. On that October night the story says that Gisli could not sleep, and neither could Aud and Gudrid. The weather was such that the air was very still—and the frost, also, was heavy. Gisli says that he wants to go from the house to his hiding-place, which was southwards under the cliffs, and see if he might sleep there. All three of them go, and they are wearing long kirtles, and the kirtles trail in the white frost. Gisli is carrying a stick and cutting runes in it, and the chips fall to the ground. They come to the hiding-place. He lies down to see if he can get some sleep; and the women stay awake. Drowsiness comes on him, and he dreams that big birds come into the place, bigger than cock-ptarmigans; and they screeched horribly; and they had been wallowing in blood. Then Aud asked him what he had been dreaming.

'My dreams are no better than before.' He spoke a verse:

> *'Loud in my mind, lady,*
> *Linen goddess, din came,*
> *Pierced me when we parted—*
> *I pour the dwarfs' liquor.*
> *Heard this tree of hard edge*
> *Hatred, fighting great birds,*
> *Beating wings. My bow's dew*
> *Will blight the hearts of fighters.'*

While he is talking they hear the sound of men's voices, and Eyjolf has come up with fourteen men, and they have been to the steading first and seen the trails over the frost, as if pointing the way. When Gisli and the two women become aware of the men they climb up on the cliffs to where the vantage is best, and the women each carry a big club. Eyjolf and his men come below.

Eyjolf spoke then to Gisli: 'It will not be right now for you to run away, and let yourself be chased like a coward, because you are called a great hero. We have not had many meetings, and we would like it if this might be the last.'

Gisli answers: 'Come at me like a man, for I shall not run any farther away. And it is for you to attack me first, because you have more against me than the other men who are here in your party.'

'I shall not leave it to you,' says Eyjolf, 'to place my men for me.'

'It was more likely,' says Gisli, 'that your dog's heart would be afraid to cross weapons with me.'

Eyjolf spoke then to spying Helgi: 'You would make a great name for yourself if you were the first to go up the cliff at Gisli, and the fame of it would go about for a long while.'

'I have seen for myself,' says Helgi, 'that you will mostly have others in front of you, where there is some danger; but because you egg me on so hard I shall do as you say, but you must come right after me, and be next man up, if you are not all a coward.'

Helgi starts upwards where the way seems best to him, and he has a big axe in his hand. Gisli's arms were an axe, which he held in his hand, and a girded sword and a shield by his side; and he was wearing a grey, cowled cloak which he had tied round himself with a cord. Helgi takes a run and springs up the cliff at Gisli. He turns to meet Helgi, swings back his sword and brings it down across his loins, so that he cuts the man in two, and the parts fall back off the cliff.

Eyjolf follows up by another way, but Aud was facing him, and she strikes his arm with her club so that all the strength goes out of it, and he falls back down. Then says Gisli: 'I knew long ago that I was well wived, but I did not know until now how well. And yet the help you have just given me is less than you hoped and expected to give me, even though your blow was good, because I would have sent both of those men the same way.'

35

TWO MEN THEN go up to hold Aud and Gudrid, and they think they have as much as they can do. Twelve men attack Gisli up on the cliffs. But he holds them off with stones and weapons so well that his defence has become famous. One of Eyjolf's fellows jumps forward and says: 'Let me have those good weapons you are holding, and your wife Aud along with them.'

Gisli answers: 'You will have to win them hard; because you are not good enough for them, neither the weapons that have been mine nor my wife.'

This man thrusts at Gisli with his spear. But Gisli strikes the spear-head from the shaft, and the blow is so heavy that the axe comes down on the flat rock beneath him and a corner snaps off from its edge. He throws down the axe then and draws his sword and fights with it, guarding himself with his shield. Now they attack manfully; and he defends himself well and with spirit; and they battled fiercely. Gisli killed another two men, and now four of them are dead. Eyjolf tells them to go at him like men—'It is not easy for us,' says Eyjolf, 'but what does that matter if the reward is good?'

Then, when it is least expected, Gisli turns about and runs across to a lone bluff called Einhamar, away from the cliffs; and there he makes his stand to defend himself. This took them unawares; and it now seems to them they they are much worse off —four men dead and the rest wounded and tired. There comes a lull in the attacking. Then Eyjolf eggs on his men harder than ever, and promises them big rewards if they will close in on Gisli. These were picked men that he had with him, for their determination and toughness.

36

A MAN CALLED Svein is the first to come at Gisli. Gisli strikes at him and splits him to the shoulders, and flings him down over the bluff. They hardly seem to know where the slaughter inflicted by this man will stop.

Gisli spoke then to Eyjolf: 'By my will, you would never earn anything more dearly than the sixty ounces of silver you have taken on my head; and what is more, I will make you wish that you could give another sixty ounces that we had never met, for you will be disgraced for losing so many men.'

Now they search for an opening, and they will not turn away after this, not for their lives. They attack him from two sides, and two are in front with Eyjolf, one called Thorir and the other Thord, kinsmen of Eyjolf; these were two hard-fighting kind of men; and the thrusting is now fierce and quick, and they succeed in wounding him in some places with their spears; but he fights back fearlessly, and with great spirit. And they take so much from him by stones and great blows that not one of them was unwounded who attacked him; for Gisli's aim was sure when he struck. They attack him fiercely, Eyjolf and his kinsmen; they saw that their honour was at stake. They wound him then with their spears, so that his bowels begin to come out; and he gathers the bowels in with his shirt and ties them underneath with the cord. Then Gisli told them to wait a little—'You will finish up the case as you want to'. He spoke a verse:

> '*Sheer goddess of shower*
> *Of spear-shaft's hall, cheer-heart,*
> *Brave, bids of her lover,*
> *Bold one, the cold tidings.*
> *Fain am I though finely*
> *Forged bright edges bite me;*
> *My sire's true sword temper,*
> *Shows in his son's life-close.*

This is Gisli's last verse; and as soon as he had spoken the verse, he leaps down from the bluff and drives his sword into the skull of Thord, Eyjolf's kinsman, and splits him right down to the middle; with this Gisli falls over on top of him, and is lifeless. And they were all badly wounded, Eyjolf's fellows.

Gisli died of so many great wounds that there seemed to be something strange about it. His attackers said that he never gave ground, and they could not see that his last blow was weaker than his first. Thus Gisli's life comes to an end, and it is everywhere agreed that he was the most valiant of men, and yet he was not in all things a lucky man. They drag his body down and take away his sword; they bury him there among the stones and go down to the sea. A sixth man died beside the water.

Eyjolf asked Aud if she wanted to go with him. But she did not want to. After this they go home to Otradal, and that same night the seventh man died. An eighth is laid up by his wounds for a year and then dies of them. The rest recover, those who had been wounded, but they have gained nothing but dishonour. And it is everywhere agreed that never in this country has one man put up a more famous defence, so far as such things can be known for certain.

37

EYJOLF GOES AWAY to the south with eleven men to visit Bork the stout, and he told him his news, and how it all happened. This put Bork in high spirits, and he tells Thordis to give Eyjolf a good welcome—'and remember how much you loved my brother Thorgrim, and do well for Eyjolf'.

'I must grieve for Gisli my brother,' says Thordis: 'and is it not enough for Gisli's killer if a pot of porridge is put before him?'

And in the evening, when she brought the food in, she lets fall the tray of spoons. Eyjolf had put between the bench and his legs the sword which had been Gisli's. Thordis recognizes the sword, and when she bends down to pick up the spoons she takes it by the hilt and thrusts it at Eyjolf, meaning to strike him in the middle. She did not heed the turn-up of the guard, which caught against the table; the blade went in lower than she intended, and cut into his thigh and made a bad wound. Bork seizes Thordis and twists the sword from her hand.

They all spring up and turn over the tables and the food. Bork asked Eyjolf to make a self-judgment for this, and he demanded full atonement, as if for the death of a man, and says he would have demanded more if Bork had not behaved so well.

Thordis names witnesses and declares herself divorced from Bork, and says that she will not come again in the same bed with him; and she kept her word. She went then to live at Thordis's steading out on the headland called Eyr.

Bork stayed on at Helgafell until Snorri godi got him out of there. Then he went to live at Glerarskogar.

Eyjolf rides home, not at all pleased with the way his visit has turned out.

38

THE SONS OF Vestein make their way to Gest, their kinsman, and ask him if he can arrange to get them away from Iceland, and their mother Gunnhild, and Aud, who had been Gisli's wife, and Gudrid, Ingjald's daughter, and her brother Geirmund. They sail from Hvita. Gest got them away at his expense. They were a short while at sea and came to Norway. Berg goes up the road and tries to find them a place to lodge in the town, and two companions were with him. They meet two men, and one of them was dressed in fine clothes, a young man and of big build; this one asked Berg his name. He told him the truth about his name and kin; because he expected that in most places he would be more likely to benefit by his father's name than suffer. But the one who was in the fine clothes drew his sword and struck Berg his death-blow. He was Ari, son of whey-Thorbjorn and brother of Gisli and Thorkell.

Berg's companions went back to the ship and told what had happened. The skipper got them away, and had Helgi taken on a ship that was going to Greenland. Helgi got there, and prospered in the country, and was respected as a fine man; and men were sent to kill him, but he was not to die this way. He perished on a fishing expedition, and this was thought a great loss.

Aud and Gunnhild went to Denmark, to Hedeby, and they became Christians there and went on pilgrimage to Rome, and did not return. Geirmund stayed on in Norway, and he married, and did well. His sister Gudrid was married, and she was thought to be a clever woman, and many people are descended from her.

Ari, whey-Thorbjorn's son, went to Iceland. He landed in Hvita and sold his ship and bought land at Hamar and lived there for some years. Then he lived on several farms in Myrar, and there are men who trace their descent from him.

We close here the story of Gisli, the son of whey-Thorbjorn.

Some Notes
on the Verses

THE *dróttkvætt*, or court metre, in which all but six of the verses were composed, makes use of a rigid pattern of alliteration, half rhyme and full rhyme. Its rhythmic unit is developed from the Germanic half line, with three instead of two stressed syllables, and having the third foot always of the falling or trochaic type. There are four pairs of these half lines in a stanza, joined by the alliteration; the first stave of the second half line is the head stave of the pair, and it always carries the alliteration. There is half rhyme in the first half line of each pair, with the last stressed syllable making one of the rhyming couple (always in the Icelandic, often in the English); full rhyme is similarly placed in the second half line. Each half line normally contains six syllables. The following translated stanza will serve as illustration; the alliteration is marked by bold, the half and full rhymes by italic:

> I **f**ought a lone **f**ateful
> **F**ight, this was my **n**ightmare;
> **S**ingle, not soon I was
> **S**lain by their main power.
> **G**ood **f**lesh by my **g**ashing
> **G**ave I mouths of ravens,
> **B**ut in your white **b**osom
> **B**right blood drops fell ruddy.

The second verse on p. 36 differs in having the alliteration but full end rhyme instead of internal rhyme.

The syntax of the verse translations is difficult and sometimes ambiguous. The kennings and a few other expressions are elucidated in the following notes:

p. 19b, *oak of herbs:* woman. Kennings for men and women often have a word for tree as their base-word.

p. 20, *snake-plot goddess:* goddess of gold, woman. Names of gods and goddesses are often used as base-words in kennings. The legendary resting place of a serpent, or dragon, was a bed of gold.

p. 24, *ship-tree:* man (here Thorgrim).

p. 26, *Giant-bane Grim:* here, as in the Icelandic, the personal name itself is concealed in a kenning, literally: troll-friend's destroyer-grim. The friend of the troll-woman is the giant, whose destroyer is the god Thor. It is of course his name which forms the first element in the dead man's name: Thorgrim. *god of war-blade gleaming:* god of the sword, warrior, man (here Thorgrim). *wearer of grim war mask:* warrior, man (Thorgrim).

p. 28, *wife-veil-hearted wavering:* the Icelandic talks of 'my sister, heedful of marriage headdress'. Thordis heeds her ties with her husband more than her ties with her brother, Gisli, and he compares her unfavourably with Gudrun, the wife of Sigurd the dragon-slayer (now known to most people through Wagner and William Morris), the Kriemhilt of the *Nibelungenlied.* Sigurd was slain by her brothers, on whom she could not take vengeance. Her second marriage was to Atli, king of the Huns, who treacherously killed her brothers in order to win the treasure they had obtained on Sigurd's death. For this Gudrun slew Atli, after first feasting him on the flesh of his dead sons.

p. 32, *unthewed:* the word *thew* is used with its old meaning in mind, custom or habit, especially a good habit or virtue.

p. 33, *land of the wave fire:* wave fire is gold, whose land is a woman.

p. 34a, *band goddess:* woman. *spender:* (generous) man. *storm tamer, treader of sword weather:* warrior, man. The Icelandic has a kenning here which goes: ruler of the wind of the Skjoldungs (an early Danish dynasty, great in legend), ruler of battle.

p. 34b, *waster of wave fire:* waster of gold, (generous) man.

p. 34c, *ring-speeder:* (generous) man.

p. 36a, *thread-work goddess:* woman. *ale goddess:* woman. *linker of strong letters:* poet. The Icelandic here has: payer-out of poetry.

p. 36b, *slaughter's gilt:* blood. The Icelandic has no kenning here. *wound flood:* blood.

p. 36c, *trees of the spear's greeting:* trees of battle, warriors, men. *wealth goddess:* woman. *seekers of sark's hatred:* the hatred of the sark, or coat of mail, is the sword, the sword's seekers are warriors, men. *strife gods:* warriors, men. The Icelandic has: wakers of strife of weapons.

p. 40, *I pour the dwarfs' liquor:* I make poetry, cf. the story told on p. xii. *tree of the sea's fire:* tree of gold, woman.

p. 47, *battle ice:* sword.

p. 48a, *goddess of threads:* woman. *praise-rune maker:* poet. The Icelandic has praise-adorner. *golden one, of seagull's ground:* woman. Probably seagull's ground, i.e. the sea, is a half-kenning for gold, stemming from a full kenning for gold of the type, fire of the sea.

p. 48b, *sea-flame goddess:* goddess of gold, woman. *linen goddess:* woman.

p. 48c, *adder's earth:* gold.

p. 50, *lords of masted fjord-elks:* lords of ships, men.

p. 52a, *bowl goddess:* woman.

p. 52b, *froth of fires of Othin:* Othin, god of battle, his fires are swords, whose froth is blood. *goddess . . . of hawk-track fire:* woman. The hawk-track is the place of the hawk or falcon, i.e. the hand, whose fire is gold. *sword-loosed tides:* blood. The Icelándic has no kenning here. *wound rain:* blood.

p. 52c, *sword rain:* blood. *thread-work goddess:* woman.

p. 53c, *crow feeder:* warrior. The Icelandic has a kenning for 'the rest' in line 2: comforters of the early flyer, i.e. the raven, on which the one in the English is based. *corpse-stream hawk:* hawk of blood, raven.

p. 54a, *wound flood:* blood. *necklet goddess:* woman. The Icelandic has: gold-wearing goddess.

p. 54b, *gods of slain net:* warriors. The Icelandic has corpse net, which is taken to mean shield. *ring goddess:* woman. *corpse-stream eagle's eye-delight providers:* warriors, who give delight to the eye of the eagle of blood, the carrion bird. The Icelandic has here the simpler kenning: nourishers of carrion fowl.

p. 54c, *shield troll-woman wielders:* warriors, men who wield the troll-woman, the malevolent enemy, of the shield, i.e. the sword. *thread goddess:* woman.

p. 55a, *band goddess:* woman. *belt goddess:* woman. *sea-fire goddess:* goddess of gold, woman.

p. 55b, *linen goddess:* woman. *I pour the dwarfs' liquor:* I make poetry, cf. p. xii. *tree of hard edge hatred:* tree of battle, warrior. The Icelandic here has: tree of the sword-voice. *bow's dew:* arrows.

p. 58, *goddess of shower of spear-shaft's hall:* goddess of gold, woman. Gold is the shower or rain of the hand; the hand is the hall or home of the spear-shaft.

Notes on the Text

For the location and topography of places in Iceland, reference should be made to the maps and plans.

Page 1

King Hakon   ruled *c.* 946–64. He was the youngest son of Harald Fairhair, the first king to rule a united Norway, and he was brought up at the court of King Athelstan of Wessex, who reigned 925–939. The Icelandic annals say that King Hakon ruled 933–61, and that whey-Thorbjorn came to Iceland in 952 (see ch. 4).

Thorkell skerauki   the nickname literally means 'rock-increment'; it is a word known on the west coast of Norway, used for the lower of two adjacent rocks which is covered at flood-tide, while its higher companion stays uncovered at all times.

Fibuli   now Årvågsfjord; see map 1.

berserk   a man capable of fits of frenzy, which increased his strength and made him regardless of pain; such men were often considered to have magical powers, and as warriors they were both prized and feared. The name 'bear-shirt' is probably due to the fact that such men regarded the bear as a kind of totem animal, and they may have dressed themselves as bears. A warrior clothed from head to foot in what appears to be a bearskin is portrayed on a woven tapestry found in the ninth-century Oseberg ship burial, see *Viking*, IV (1940), 104, fig. 7 (*a*). Medically it is thought that berserks were paranoiac and perhaps sometimes epileptic, sensitive to suggestion and auto-suggestion, so that they could fall, either at will or under the right stimulus, into a violent fury strictly similar to the running amuck of the Malays and other comparatively primitive peoples. As a mental disease it may be related to lycanthropy—it may well have been that some berserks, when the fit was on them, really believed that they were changed into bears. Alcohol may sometimes have played a part in producing the berserk mood, but it is not thought that other stimulants were used. (It has been suggested that the poisonous type of toadstool, *Amanita muscaria*, was used to call forth the berserk fury, but this plant, used as an intoxicant by some East Siberian tribes, has toxicological effects which only in uncommon instances agree with descriptions of the berserk fury.) See F. Grøn, *Berserksgangens vesen og årsaksforhold* (Det kgl. Norske Videnskabers Selskabs Skrifter, 1929, Nr 4; Trondheim, 1929); with a summary in German.

In the sagas berserks are stock figures in situations like the one described here.

Greyflank names were often given to prized weapons, sometimes to mail-coats as well; weapons with magical attributes are common in folktales. The Icelandic name of the weapon is *Grásíða*, which cannot originally have been a sword name, because it is a feminine word—all other sword names are masculine. The name belongs to the spear into which this sword is forged later in the story (ch. 11), and to the real spear that was in use in the thirteenth century, see the Essay, p. 129 below.

Page 2

and both a possible model for this story about the death
men die of the elder Gisli may be found in a tradition connected with a member of the family of

Aud, wife of the younger Gisli in Iceland. See the anecdote told of Vegest, Aud's uncle, and the thrall Bjorn, in the *Book of the Settlements*, translated on p. 87 below.

Stokkar identified as Stokke in Valsøyfjord; see map 1. Stokkaholm, mentioned earlier, is probably a small island in the narrow sound dividing the mainland where Stokke lies from the larger island Valsøy.

Fridarey the island Frei; see map 1.

Hella possibly to be identified with Mjølkill in Øksendal or Helle in Vistdal, Romsdal; see map 1.

Page 3

Grannaskeid identified as Skei; see map 1.

Saxa not identified; it has been suggested that it is really a weapon's name, a spear or preferably an axe, and that its identification as a place name in the saga is due to a misunderstanding of the couplet 'Warflame whistled', p. 4. But we cannot account for the origin of the verse any more than for the name itself. If it is a place name in the verse, we have an example of the 'pathetic fallacy', not unknown elsewhere in early Norse poetry.

duelling rules the word for duel is *hólmganga*, literally 'island-going', since duels were traditionally fought on islands, perhaps because they were often a no man's land where blood might be shed with impunity, or perhaps because they had ready-made limits which made escape or interference difficult. There seem to have been two main forms of single combat, a free-for-all (*einvígi*) and the formal duel (*hólmganga*), although the two terms are not always kept distinct. Many duels are described in the sagas, but the only elaborate account of the rules is in *Kormáks saga*, ch. 10, where it says that a piece of cloth seven and a half feet square should be laid on the ground, fastened down through loops at the corners by pegs—the fixing of the pegs was a ritual act. Around this on each side three furrows, each a foot wide, were to be drawn, and outside these four hazel-posts (probably joined by a rope) were to be fixed. The technical expression in the Icelandic, *hasla völl*, means 'to hazel the field', and refers to the placing of the hazel-posts (translated here as 'challenges Kolbjorn by marking out the ring'), but later seems to have the general sense 'appoint a battle-place'. Each duellist was allowed three shields, but when they had been hacked useless he had to rely on his weapons only. The duellist had a second who protected him with the shield (but not here in the saga of Gisli). The challenger had to receive the first blow. If one of the duellists is wounded so that blood falls on the cloth, they are not obliged to continue. A man who puts one foot outside the limits set by the hazel-posts is said to retreat, but if he goes outside with both feet he is said to run. The man who is worse wounded can buy himself off from the duel by paying three marks (24 ounces) of silver.

Page 4

'and have one stand close behind the other' significant of a charge of sodomy, the worst insult. Cf. *Bjarnar saga Hítdælakappa*, ch. 17.

Flydruness not identified.

whey using whey to extinguish a fire is a motive found elsewhere, cf. e.g. *Njáls saga*, ch. 129, and for an instance from real life, *Hrafns saga Sveinbjarnarsonar*, ch. 15. Whey was kept to drink and for use as a pickling agent.

Page 5

Aesundir   the island Asen; see map 1.

whey- in Icelandic Thorbjorn *súrr*, and Gisli is called
Thorbjorn Súrsson, the nickname replacing the birth-
name. The nickname *súrr* is doubtless derived
from the place name Surnadal, where Thorbjorn came from, and has nothing to do with
whey. The inhabitants of Surnadal were
called *Súrdælir*.

Page 6

buried in a in Norway it had been customary for centuries
mound to build mounds over the graves of distinguished persons. No cremation graves have
been found in Iceland, but by the tenth
century inhumation was also much commoner
than cremation in western Norway.

the Thing at this assembly is said to have been established
Thorsness by Thorolf Mostrarskegg (i.e. man from
Moster, an island in Sunnhordland, Norway),
who is reckoned to have come to Iceland *c.*
885. It was near the present farm called
Jónsnes, but the site was moved after a few
years to the present Þingvellir because of the
desecration of the original Thing-place; see
Eyrbyggja saga, chs. 4, 9–10.

Thorstein *Eyrbyggja saga*, ch. 11, which in this must be
cod-biter counted a reliable source, says that he died
when he was twenty-five, not more than a few
months after the birth of his son, Thorgrim,
and thus long before the events related here in
the saga of Gisli are supposed to have taken
place.

Hvalseyr another Thing in Dyrafjord was held at
Thingeyr; both of these were probably local
assemblies; the chief Thing in the West Fjords
was the Thorskafjord Thing, see ch. 28.

Page 7

the rank of a godi — on the godi and his authority, see the Essay, pp. 95–7.

dressed in coloured clothes — Icelandic cloth was usually left in the natural colours of the wool. Men returning from abroad are often described in the sagas as wearing brightly coloured foreign stuffs— counted great finery.

Gest, son of Oddleif — plays a part in several other sagas and always appears in the same guise: a man of wisdom, justice and goodwill, endowed with prophetic powers; cf. *Laxdœla saga*, ch. 33; *Njáls saga*, ch. 103; *Hávarðar saga Ísfiirðings*, chs. 7, 22–3.

booth — at the assemblies, which were held in the open air, men lived in huts called 'booths' which had permanent walls of stone and turf and were roofed for the occasion with awnings of cloth.

blood-brotherhood — a description of the ceremony is also found in *Fóstbrœðra saga*, ch. 2, where the foster-brothers are said to pass under three strips of turf raised up but with the ends still fast in the earth. The ceremony's significance is best interpreted as a rebirth from Earth, the common mother, symbolized by the passage under the raised sod and the communion of the foster-brothers' blood in the soil. The spear may have had some phallic significance. The strip of turf that was cut out must have been semicircular in outline. The ceremony has been put in its widest background by Jan de Vries, 'Der altnordische Rasengang', *Acta Philologica Scandinavica*, III (1928–9), 106–35.

Page 8

with a dama-
scened blade
the adjective 'damascened' is properly used
only of patterned steel of eastern origin, but a
similar effect was produced by Scandinavian
smiths by the process known as pattern-
welding. In this the body of the blade is
made up of alternate strips of steel and iron
welded together then split, twisted and re-
welded, before having the cutting-edges added
and the finishing treatment. A simpler and
commoner process to produce the same surface effect was to hammer the pattern-
bearing strips flat and then weld them to a core
of plain iron. See A. Liestøl, 'Blodrefill og
mål', *Viking*, XV (1951), 71–98; with illustra-
tions and an English summary. Cf. the reforging of Greyflank in ch. 11.

timber to the
value of sixteen
ounces of silver
the Icelandic expression to which this is supposed to answer is *fjögur hundruð viðar*,
literally 'four hundred of timber'. This is taken
to mean timber to the value of 480 (one hun-
dred=120) ells of homespun cloth (*vaðmál*), which *c.* 1000 were worth 16 ounces of
silver. It is possible, but less likely, that the
expression means 480 pieces of timber.
Timber seems to figure in only one price-list,
from *c.* 1200, and 480 lengths would then have
cost 20 ounces of silver.

Page 9

Harald
Greycloak
ruled Norway with his brothers after the death
of Hakon, foster-son of Athelstan, *c.* 964–74
(at the latest).

Page 10

Viborg
in the middle of Jutland, some eight miles
south of Hjarbæk fjord, which joins the great
Limfjord. As a nodal point for many routes it
early became a trading and political centre,
and its name ('sanctuary hill') shows that it
was a cult centre as well.

He made a coin the detailed description suggests that the author may have known such a token. In Norway a small triangular piece of soapstone (steatite) has been found with an inscription in runes: 'Jón gaf Heinr(ek)' (J. gave H.). It dates from *c.* 1300 and has been identified as half of such a token as the one described here, though of a much simpler kind. See Magnus Olsen, *Norges Innskrifter med de yngre Runer*, IV (1957), 257–9 (Borgund, IV); and further, V (1960), 30–1 (Trondheim, II).

Page 11

The hall the Icelandic literally translated says that the hall was '100 long and 10 fathoms wide'; and the '100' has been taken to mean fathoms, i.e. 600 feet! It is better to assume the measurement was meant to be in ells, which gives 150 feet. A man called Bjarni Skegg-Broddason built a hall in Iceland 210 feet long, 21 feet high and 21 feet wide, and was given the nickname 'house-long' (*húslangr*) in consequence. See Jakob Benediktsson, *Skarðsárbók* (1958), 190.

bower it seems to have been fairly common to have a small separate building as a work-room and sitting-room for the women, in a sheltered position as here.

cut out a shirt if a girl made clothes for a man it was a sign of her affection for him. The idea in the saga here is more clearly expressed in the Danish ballad *Marsk Stig* than anywhere else in older Icelandic literature. The Danish king comes to seduce Marsk Stig's wife:

> *Her sidder I, skønne Fru Ingeborg,*
> *og vil I være mig huld:*
> *da syr I mig en Skjorte*
> *og sinker den med røde Guld.*

Skulde jeg sy eder en Skjorte
og sinke den med røden Guld:
saa Mænd ved, Danerkongen,
da var jeg Hr. Marsti uhuld.

(*Here sit you, fair lady Ingeborg;*
if you will be loyal to me,
then sew for me a shirt
with gold embroidery.

Should I sew a shirt for you
with gold embroidery,
then men would know, Danish king,
I was disloyal to lord Marsti.)

Page 12

declare my
divorce

divorce seems to have been a comparatively easy matter in pagan times in Iceland, but the laws relating to marriage were naturally much affected by canon law after the Conversion and little is known for certain about the causes and means of divorce in the early period. The sagas seem to agree on regarding pre-Christian divorce as a legal form, consisting of a declaration to be made by either party in the presence of witnesses. A procedure is described in some detail in the *Njáls saga*, ch. 7, but nowhere else. There the wife is to declare herself divorced in the presence of witnesses at the side of her husband's bed and again in front of the main doorway of his home. The legal cause of the threatened divorce here in the saga of Gisli may, in the eyes of the author, have been Thorkel's refusal to share his bed with his wife. There is a study of the subject by C. F. von Schwerin, 'Die Ehescheidung im älteren isländischen Recht', in *Deutsche Islandforschung*, 1930, I. 283–99.

my price and
my dowry

mundr and *heimanfylgja* in the Icelandic. The first was the sum (in cash, land or chattels) paid or promised by the bridegroom at the

72

time of the marriage contract. It became the property of the wife, but was administered by the husband, although any income derived from it also went to the wife. The second was the wife's dowry, administered by the husband to his own profit, but repayable on divorce. The *heimanfylgja* was a customary payment, the *mundr* an obligatory one.

Page 13

moving-days   the time when men might legally change their residence: four days beginning on the Thursday which fell between 21st and 27th May each year.

Winter Nights   the first days of the first month of winter (the native calendar counted only two seasons, summer and winter), which began on the Saturday falling in the week 11th–17th October each year. This was a time for one of the biggest pagan festivals (it coincided with the autumn slaughtering of cattle), enacted however more in private cult celebrations (house-parties) than in public temple-worship. The celebrations and sacrifices made up a fertility rite, at the centre of which stood the god Frey (cf. below), accompanied by the *dísir*, female fertility deities, led by Freyja (according to the mythology she was Frey's sister and wife). See Folke Ström, *Diser, Norner, Valkyrjor* (1954); with a summary in German.

Gisli no longer sacrificed   it is implied that Gisli had come under Christian influence in Viborg. This would have been quite possible chronologically, because Christian missionaries were active in Denmark in the middle of the tenth century and they usually began their work in important townships.

Page 15

the Bandvettir   the name means a pair of mittens attached to each other by a string.

Page 16

a tapestry   the word *refill* in the Icelandic seems to have meant a long narrow strip of woven material with pictures worked in it. When a hall was hung with tapestries, it seems that the walls were covered by large pieces of cheaper cloth, plain or with a simple pattern, over which the richer *refill* was displayed. Such narrow picture-tapestries were found in the ninth-century Oseberg ship burial, only some six to nine inches in width. See Bjørn Hougen, 'Osebergfunnets billedvev', *Viking*, IV (1940), 85–124. The width of the Bayeux Tapestry is fifty centimetres.

Page 17

Thorkell, his oath-brother   it appears from this that the failure of the blood-brotherhood ceremony was not regarded as complete: Thorgrim refused to clinch the matter with Vestein and Gisli refused to do it with Thorgrim, but the bonds between Gisli, Thorkell and Vestein were rightly established. There were thus no oaths to prevent Thorgrim's slaying of Vestein and Gisli's slaying of Thorgrim.

tells him to take the weapon from the wound   Aud's intention seems to be to keep Gisli out of trouble. There seems to be no parallel to the rule stated here that the man who took the weapon from a wound was obliged to avenge that wound; neither is the distinction made here between secret manslaughter and murder known in other sources. The distinction between manslaughter (*víg*) and murder (*morð*) was that the former was a slaying publicly declared by the slayer, while the latter was one that was kept secret, either by hiding the corpse or by the failure of the slayer to acknowledge his act. There may be some substance in what the saga says about secret manslaughter, if we presume that the weapon left in the wound was usually recognizable as

74

the slayer's property; but this could scarcely apply here, because Greyflank in its new shape was an unknown weapon. It is different when Gisli uses it on Thorgrim.

Page 18

He had Vestein's body got ready for burial mouth and nose were closed and possibly the eyes; the body may have been washed and the head wrapped in or covered by a cloth.

Hel-shoes it is a common and ancient belief that the dead man has a long journey before him and needs good shoes: graves of Greeks and Alemanni, for example, have been found with shoes in them; in some parts of Germany the funeral feast has been called *Totenschuh*. See Dag Strömbäck, 'Att binda helskor', *Kungl. Hum. Vetenskaps-Samfundet i Uppsala, Årsbok*, 1952, 139–48. It has been suggested that Thorgrim's intention here was to make Vestein's journey to the home of the dead as easy as possible; and once there he could not return (much of the usual treatment of the dead was designed to prevent any reanimation of the corpse). Valhall was Odin's hall, a paradise for warriors, who fought there by day and feasted by night—it seems to be a late, Viking Age, conception of the after-life. We mostly hear of the dead joining their ancestors, sometimes inside a hill or mountain regarded as sacred, or of a shadowy and miserable realm of the dead, ruled over by the goddess Hel, in origin doubtless a generalized extension of the ancient communal grave.

Page 19

'I dreamt a dream,' says Gisli according to the opening of the chapter, Gisli's dreams were on the two nights before the night of Vestein's slaying, not on that night and the one before.

a viper . . . a wolf neither animal is found in Iceland but they are the classical Scandinavian embodiments of the beasts foe to men. Two of the monsters who are to bring about the doom of the pagan gods are the World-serpent, *Miðgarðsormr*, and the great wolf, *Fenrir*. As symbols of evil they are associated with witches: a witch-woman is described as riding a wolf with a snake for reins, and a figure is pictured in this way on one of the Hunnestad-stones in Skåne, carved in the first half of the eleventh century; see the illustration in L. Wimmer, *Danmarks Rune-mindesmærker*, III, 28. Wolves often appear in dreams described in the sagas, usually symbolizing approaching enemies; cf. ch. 33.

'And I have not told either dream before now . . .' the belief that dreams turn out according to their interpretation is known in modern times in Iceland. See Jónas Jónasson, *Íslenzkir þjóðhættir* (1945), 415.

Page 20

sports these are to show that the two households are on friendly terms. The game played was the ball-game, events in which are described in chs. 15 and 18. No complete description of the game is found anywhere, but it seems to have been played between pairs from different teams. The object was to get the ball over the opponent's base-line, and the game seems to have been opened by the one with the bat hitting the ball towards his opponent's line (it is not certain whether they each had a bat); thereafter both chased the ball and there were no rules as to the means whereby one circumvented the opponent. The game was most often played on flat frozen surfaces, as here on the frozen pond. Trouble often arises from games and horse-fights in the sagas, but they must have sometimes ended peacefully as well. The ball-game was rough enough, but doubtless enjoyable when one was used to it.

Page 21

a sacrifice
to Frey

Frey was pre-eminently a god of fertility (cf. the note on p. 73 on the Winter Nights). We may note the brief contemporary evidence of Adam of Bremen who, writing *c.* 1070, describes the images of Thor, Odin and Frey in the great temple in Uppsala. Of the last he says: 'Tercius est Fricco, pacem voluptatemque largiens mortalibus. Cuius etiam simulacrum fingunt cum ingenti priapo.' Frey is mentioned in several other sagas as the 'patron' of individuals and families, see especially *Víga-Glúms saga* and *Hrafnkels saga Freysgoða*.

Eyjolf
Thordsson

called 'the grey', a member of one of the most important families in the west of Iceland and an ancestor of Ari Thorgilsson the Learned (1067–1148), Iceland's first historian and prose-writer. In his *Íslendingabók* Ari says that Eyjolf was baptized in his old age when Iceland was converted to Christianity (A.D. 1000). He was a cousin of Bork and Thorgrim, Eyjolf's father being the brother of their mother. Little is told of him in other sources. His nickname 'grey' suggests 'the guileful', but we cannot be certain of this. In *Njáls saga*, ch. 138, it is said of a grandson of his that 'he was avaricious like the rest of his kinsfolk', which may well be a reflection of Eyjolf's presentation in the *Gísla saga*.

Page 23

a blue cape

in other sagas it is said that men wore blue clothes when they were bent on killing (e.g. *Víga-Glúms saga*, ch. 8; *Hrafnkels saga*, chs. 3, 8; *Laxdœla saga*, ch. 87), but in ch. 20, p. 29, it says that Gisli usually wore a blue cape. Ian Maxwell plausibly suggests that the idea is that for an important job a man wears his best clothes.

Page 23

bed closet   principal members of a household often had
their beds in a small panelled bed closet, which
could be shut by a door fastening on the
inside; other members of the household slept
on the raised plank flooring that ran most of
the length of the hall-walls on each side, which
was also the place to sit by day.

Page 25

and lay Thor-   boat- and ship-graves are well known in
grim in a boat   Scandinavia and elsewhere and are sometimes
mentioned in the sagas. Three certain boat-
graves, and one uncertain, have been found in
Iceland. The two boats found in graves at
Dalvík in Svarfaðardalur (middle north coast
of Iceland) were of decent size: approximate
length 21 feet, 22 feet 9 inches, beam 3 feet
9 inches, 4 feet 10 inches, respectively. See
Kristján Eldjárn, *Kuml og haugfé* (1956), 212–
218. A tenth-century grave at Vendel (Upp-
land, Sweden) contained a boat some 30 feet
long, in which towards the stern a single large
stone, about a yard long and a foot wide, had
been placed. Another grave from the same
period, found at Storedal (Smaalenene, south-
east of the Oslofjord), contained a smaller
boat, 13–16 feet long, which also had a single
stone in it, measuring about a foot each way.
No other stones were found in either of these
boats or in either of the mounds heaped over
them. See J. Petersen, 'Overtro fra gravhaug',
Maal og minne, 1914, 106–9. The royal grave-
ship from *c*. 850, excavated at Oseberg on the
west side of the Oslofjord, was moored in the
grave-mound by a large stone, attached to a
rope-cable running from the starboard side of
the prow; inside the vessel a light and handsome anchor was found. See H. Shetelig, Hj.
Falk and E. V. Gordon, *Scandinavian Archae-
ology* (1937), plate 46 (p. 282) and plate 57*b*
(p. 358).

a spell *seiðr* in the Icelandic, a type of shamanistic magic-working, probably borrowed by the Norwegians from their Lapp neighbours, although some people think it has more ancient Germanic origins. The wizard or shaman mounted a raised platform and fell into a trance, aided normally, it seems, by a circle of singers round about the platform; he was recalled from his trance by the single song of a special singer. The purpose of the platform was to remove him from disturbing influences. While in the trance it was believed that his soul was freed and either went to seek information about the future, or, if the purpose was evil, went to 'attack' the object of the rite, whose mind and body could be enfeebled and killed. *seiðr* was not considered manly, although it is not said explicitly why in Norse sources; there are, however, numerous sexual elements in this form of magic practised till recently by Lappish and Siberian tribes, and similar elements were probably to be found in its Norse form as well. The fullest description of divinatory *seiðr* in Icelandic sources is in *Eiríks saga rauða*, ch. 4; see also *Ynglinga saga*, ch. 7 (in the *Heimskringla*). Similar to the purpose of the magic here in the *Gísla saga* is that in *Egils saga Skalla-Grímssonar*, ch. 59, where it says that Queen Gunnhild of Norway had *seiðr* performed to the end that Egill might never know peace of mind in Iceland until she had seen him again—her ultimate aim was vengeance. A classic monograph on the subject is by Dag Strömbäck, *Sejd* (Nordiska Texter och Undersökningar, 5; 1935).

the god was unwilling to have frost come between them land where the vegetation was rich or the crops always good seems often to have been regarded as specially favoured by Frey, the god of fertility. The most famous example of a 'Frey's field' in Iceland is the *Vitazgjafi*, 'the

79

giver of the assured [crop]', see *Viga-Glúms saga*, chs. 7 ff. In Sunnmøre in Norway there is a farm *Frøise* ('Frey's pasture'), where it is said that the crops never freeze. The same virtue was attributed to saints of the Christian Church. In the *Óláfs saga helga*, ch. 179 (in the *Heimskringla*), it says that St Olaf blessed the land of Grøningar and said that corn would never freeze there, even though there was frost on all the lands around. It is, however, reported that it froze there in 1877, although this was said to have been the first time for a century. See Anne Holtsmark, 'Vitazgjafi', *Studier i norrøn diktning* (1956), 38–58 (also in *Maal og Minne*, 1935).

Page 26

they changed in *Eyrbyggja saga*, ch. 12, it says that the lad
his name to was rather unruly in his youth, so they changed
Snorri his name to Snerrir, which means 'turbulent', and later called him Snorri, which is from the same root as Snerrir but was already established as a proper name. On this Snorri, cf. the Essay, p. 127, and the text, pp. 88–9.

nicknamed the blemished is *annmarki* in the Icelandic and was
blemished doubtless adopted from the place name Ann-markastadir. Many settlement names and topographical names in Iceland are compounded with personal names, and these made a rich quarry of plausible local names for tellers of tales and authors of sagas.

Page 27

withershins Cf. these sixteenth-century quotations from the *New English Dictionary*: 'Sayand the said Margarat Baffour vas ane huyr and ane wyche and that she yeid widersonnis about mennis hous sark alane.' 'Thir venerabill virginis quhome ye wald call wiches . . . nyne tymes, widersones, about the thorne raid . . .' The opposite movement, with the sun, is a safe-guard and a well-wishing. As late as 1828 in Grímsey, the remote inhabited island off the north coast of Iceland, coffin-bearers turned the coffin three times, following the course of the sun, when they came out of the church. And cf. Scott's *Waverley*, ch. 24, and a description of a drastic cure for lunacy in O. H. Mackenzie, *A Hundred Years in the Highlands* (1949), 179.

A similar story to that told here in the saga of Gisli is in *Vatnsdæla saga*, ch. 36: 'That evening when the sun was set, a shepherd saw Gro go out and she went withershins around the buildings. . . . She looked up toward the mountain and waved a cloth, in which she had tied a large gold ring of hers, and said: "Let go what is ready to go." Afterwards she went in and shut the door. Then a landslide fell on the steading and everyone there was killed.'

stoned to death the whole method of execution and burial was inspired by fear and designed to minimize the baleful power of the witch both on the point of death and after death. Stoning is 'the natural form for a collective penal action'. It was commonly used against sorcerers, partly because it was a collective action and responsi-bility was shared, and partly, perhaps, because stones were felt to possess earth's inherent magic power, more effective than weapons. (There are a number of stories in which the champion can only be overcome by stones, not by steel.) The bag over the sorcerer's head meant that his evil eye could do no harm. The execution on the foreshore between high and low water mark had a neutralizing effect: it was a no man's land, where sometimes male-factors were buried, and they were believed to be bound by the movement of the tide. Burial on the ridge between the valleys had the same intention; in land uninhabited and

indeterminate, belonging to neither settlement,
the dead could do least harm. Cf. Folke Ström,
*On the sacral origin of the Germanic death
penalties* (1942), 102–15.

Page 28

protection that may bring a case against me   technically it was an offence to give aid to an
outlaw, to help him on his way, to feed or
house him, or to take any action that might
enable him to save his life.

Page 29

summoning-days   a summons to answer a case to be brought at
the Thing was an essential legal preliminary.
It was normally made in the presence of witnesses at the home of the man to be prosecuted
and should take place as a rule a fortnight
before the Spring Thing.

summon Gisli to the Thing at Thorsness   about the same time as Gisli was outlawed a
reform in the Icelandic constitution was made.
Before then a case had to be brought at the
Thing in the locality of the man prosecuted, no
matter where the prosecutor came from. After
the reform, however, cases in which the prosecutor came from a different district were to go
to the more neutral ground of newly established Quarter Things (one for each quarter of
the country) or to the Althing. That being so,
we should probably regard the Thorsness
Thing to which Gisli was summoned as the
Quarter Thing; but our knowledge of tenth-
century Icelandic law is very limited, and it is
not certain that the author of the saga was
particularly well informed either.

homespun   this cloth (*vaðmál*) was one of Iceland's chief
products in the early period and soon became
used as a form of currency, with its value
related to that of silver (cf. the note on Thorgrim's purchase of timber, p. 70). Thorkell
presumably meant the cloth over the saddle to
prove that he really was collecting a debt, paid
part in cloth, part in silver.

Page 33

**Grettir
Asmundsson**
the most famous of all Icelandic outlaws, hero of the *Grettir saga*. He lived as an outlaw in Iceland for nineteen years, until finally killed in 1031 (or perhaps somewhat later).

seven fires
fire or flame in various forms is a common symbol of life in folk-belief and folk-tale. The verse mentions only the number of the fires, symbolizing the seven years Gisli has yet to live, and says nothing of their varying degrees of brightness. What this is supposed to signify is not made clear—presumably some good years and some bad. Cf. *Handwörterbuch des deutschen Aberglaubens*, V, 967–70, on Lebenslicht, and II, 1397, on the appearance of fire in dreams.

Page 35

Vadil
this farm is about four miles east of Hagi, the home, according to other sources, of Gest Oddleifsson, and only a little over a mile from Hvamm, Thorkell's farm. If Gisli in fact stayed at Vadil during his outlawry, it can only have been with the connivance of Gest and Thorkell.

Page 37

**Gisli takes up a
stick and cuts
runes on it**
the only writing known in heathen Scandinavia was that in the various forms of the runic alphabet. Runes were used on stone monuments, on metal and bone objects, often then with magical import, and on wood. Verses are sometimes said to have been cut on wood, and the runic art and the poetic art were often allied. Wood was of course the easiest material to work, but also the most perishable, so that very few early inscriptions on wood have been preserved. An excellent introduction to the subject of runic inscriptions is Sven B. F. Jansson, *The Runes of Sweden* (1962).

Ingjald he was not related to Gisli, but was born in Iceland, son of the Hergils after whom his island is named (see Finnur Jónsson, *Landnámabók* (1900), 39, 85, 162, 164). In ch. 38 Gudrid, foster-daughter of Gisli, is said to be daughter of an Ingjald, and in the younger version of the saga Gudrid and her brother are described, on their introduction in the story (see ch. 10), as children of Ingjald, 'kinsman of Gisli and Thorkell'. In this version of the saga it is thus made clear that the father of the children has been identified as the Ingjald of Hergilsey. It is not, however, certain that this identification was originally made in the saga. It remains evident that the author knew little about Ingjald and made him Gisli's cousin to make the story of his sheltering Gisli more convincing. Ingjald's family was a good one; his son was married to the sister of Thord Glumsson (usually Ingunnarson after his mother), second husband of Gudrun Osvifrsdottir, the famous heroine of the *Laxdœla saga*.

Page 39

Vadsteinaberg it is said that this eminence is not a good place for defence, because attackers might approach on three sides, There is also nothing on the island which might be reasonably described as 'a little dale' (see the beginning of ch. 27). The author seems never to have been ashore on Hergilsey.

Page 44

Hallbjorn, a tramp in the laws it says that if a man takes to the road and accepts alms for a fortnight or more, or takes his lodging where he can find it, then he is a vagabond. An able-bodied man who turned tramp was liable to outlawry, and vagabonds in general were severely treated, enjoying little or no legal protection. But the law can hardly have been severely enforced, for elsewhere in the laws we learn that vagabonds might have booths at the Althing, since it says that if such men misbehaved there, their booths might be destroyed with impunity.

Page 46

of calling myself by another name Gest is apparently suggesting that the boys were not really the sons of Vestein but had only pretended to be, in order to create legal confusion if the slaying were followed up. The writer does not make it very plausible.

he was tied to them by kinship we have no means of knowing whether this is true or not.

Page 59

until Snorri godi got him out of there that is, his nephew Snorri, son of Thorgrim and Thordis, see ch. 18 above. How Snorri got Bork out of Helgafell is told in *Eyrbyggja saga*, ch. 14.

Page 60

to Denmark, to Hedeby the biggest and most important of all Scandinavian trading towns in the Viking Age, in existence from at least *c.* 800. The town-site covered some sixty-five acres and lay near the present town of Schleswig (now German), some twenty miles north-west of Kiel; soon after 1050 it was moved to Schleswig itself. A church was built in Hedeby *c.* 850, by St Ansgar.

many people are descended from her nothing is known of people descended from Gudrid—presuming her existence was real in the first place.

Ari, whey-Thorbjorn's son his existence is extremely doubtful; nothing is known otherwise of any settlement by him or of any men who trace their descent from him.

Extracts from Other Sources

The settlement in Arnarfjord and Dyrafjord

THIS ACCOUNT IS taken from the recension of the *Book of the Settlements* known as *Hauksbók*. This was made about 1300, but its text in this part is thought to represent the older recension, *Styrmisbók*, made before 1245, better than does the other early extant recension, *Sturlubók* (*c.* 1260). The original texts will be found in Finnur Jónsson, *Landnámabók*, I-III (1900), 44-6, 168-70. The names of people who figure in the saga of Gisli are printed bold. In this translation the genealogies have been cut short at about 1200.

There was a famous man called Orn. He went from Rogaland because of King Harald's tyranny. He took the whole of Arnarfjord. He stayed the winter on Tjaldaness, because the sun did not leave this place at the winter solstice.

An red-cloak, son of Grim hairy-cheek from Hrafnista and of Helga, daughter of An bow-bender, got on bad terms with King Harald, and because of that he left the country to go raiding in the west. He made attacks on Ireland and there he married Grelod, daughter of Earl Bjartmar. They went to Iceland and arrived in Arnarfjord a year later than Orn. An spent the first winter in Dufansdal. Grelod thought the ground gave out a bad smell there. Orn heard that his kinsman, Hamund dark-skin, was north in Eyjafjord, so he sold all the lands between Langaness and Stapi to An red-cloak. An made his homestead at Eyr. Grelod thought the grass there smelt like honey. An gave Dufansdal to his thrall Dufan. **Bjartmar** was the son of An; he was father of the two Vegests and of **Helgi**, whose daughters were Thurid and Arnkatla. Thorhild was the daughter of Bjartmar who was married to **Vestein Vegeirsson**, and their children were

Aud and **Vestein.** Hjallkar was a freeman of An's. His son was Bjorn, who was a thrall of Bjartmar's. Bjartmar gave him his freedom. Then he made money. Vegest made trouble about this and thrust Bjorn through with a spear, but Bjorn hit him with a hoe and killed him.

Geirthjof Valthjofsson also took land in Arnarfjord: Forsfjord, Reykjarfjord, Trostansfjord, Geirthjofsfjord, and all the way to Langaness, and he lived in Geirthjofsfjord. He was married to Salgerd, daughter of Ulf the squinter. Their son was Hogni, father of Atli, father of Hoskuld, father of Atli, father of Bard the black, father of Sveinbjorn, father of Hrafn.

A man named Eirik took Keldudal south of Dyrafjord and Slettaness as far as Stapi in Arnarfjord and as far as outer Hals in Dyrafjord. He was the father of **Thorkell,** father of Thord, father of Thorkell, father of Steinolf, father of Thord, father of Thorleif, mother of Thorgerd, mother of Thora, mother of Gudmund pig, who was married to Solveig, daughter of Jon Loptsson.

Vestein, son of Vegeir and brother of Vebjorn, champion of the Sogn-men, took land between the Halsar in Dyrafjord and lived in Haukadal. He was married to Thorhild, daughter of Bjartmar. **Whey-Thorbjorn** came out to Iceland when the land had all been taken up. Vestein gave him half of Haukadal. His children were **Gisli,** who was married to **Aud, Vestein's daughter,** and **Thorkell,** who was married to Sigrid, daughter of Slettu-Bjorn, and **Thordis,** whom **Thorgrim Thorsteinsson** had to wife.[1] Their son was **Snorri the Chieftain.**

Dyri was the name of a man [2] who went from Sunnmøre to Iceland on the advice of Earl Rognvald.[3] He took Dyrafjord and lived at Halsar. His son was Hrafn, who lived at Ketilseyr, father of Thurid, who was married to **Vestein Vesteinsson.** Their sons were **Berg** and **Helgi.**

Thord was the name of a man, son of Viking—most men say that Viking was a son of King Harald Fairhair. Dyri gave Thord land between Thufa on Hjallaness and Jardfallsgil, and he lived in Alvidra. He was married to Thjodhild, sister of Helgi the lean. Their son was the champion, **Thorkell the rich,** who lived there

---

[1] In *Sturlubók* the name of Thorkell's wife is not given; Ari is added as a son of whey-Thorbjorn; and Thordis's second marriage, to Bork the stout, is also mentioned.

[2] *Sturlubók* calls him a famous man.

[3] *Sturlubók* adds: and because of the tyranny of King Harald Fairhair.

afterwards. His sons were Thord the left-handed and Eyjolf, father of the Gisli who was married to Hallgerd, daughter of Vermund the slender. Their son was Brand, father of the priest Gudmund in Hjardarholt, father of the priest Magnus. Another son of Thord Vikingsson was Thorvald the white. He was married to Thora Knjuk's daughter. Their son was Thord the white or the left-handed, who was married to Asdis Thormod's daughter, the mother of Ulf the marshal. Thord the left-handed's daughter was Ottkatla, wife of Sturla Thjodreksson. Their son was Thord who was married to Hallbera, daughter of Snorri the Chieftain. Sturla's daughter was Asny, wife of Snorri Jorundsson. Their daughter was Thordis, mother of Hoskuld the physician, father of Margaret, mother of Abbot Thorfinn.

Life of Snorri the Chieftain

On this record see the Essay, pp. 100 and 127.

Snorri the Chieftain had nineteen freeborn children who lived beyond childhood. Thord kitten was the eldest, second Thorodd, third Thorstein, fourth Gudlaug the monk; these were sons of Asdis, Viga-Styr's daughter; the fifth was Sigrid, the sixth Unn; these were daughters of Thurid, Illugi the red's daughter; seventh was Klepp, eighth Halldora, ninth Thordis, tenth Gudrun, eleventh Halldor, twelfth Mani, thirteenth Eyjolf, fourteenth Thora, fifteenth Hallbera, sixteenth Thurid, seventeenth Thorleif, eighteenth Alof, nineteenth Snorri; this Snorri was born after his father's death; these were children of Hallfrid Einar's daughter. Snorri the Chieftain had three children born of bondwomen: another Thord kitten was one, and Jorund and Thorhild.

Snorri the Chieftain was fourteen years old when he went abroad; he was abroad one winter. The winter following his return he lived at Helgafell with Bork the stout, his father's brother, and Thordis, his mother. This same autumn Eyjolf the grey, son of Thord bellower, killed Gisli, son of whey-Thorbjorn, and in the following spring, when Snorri was sixteen years old, he began to farm Helgafell, and he lived there for twenty [1] years before Christianity was made law in Iceland and another eight years after that, and during the last winter he was there Thorgest

---

[1] Corrected from twenty-three.

Thorhallsson killed Viga-Styr, Snorri the Chieftain's father-in-law, at Jorvi in Flisuhverfi. Afterwards he moved to Sælingsdals-tunga and lived there for twenty-three [1] years. He had a church built at Helgafell, and another at Tunga in Sælingsdal; and some people say that he joined with Gudrun in building a second church at Helgafell, when the one he had built there himself burnt down. He died of sickness in the sixty-seventh year of his age; that was one winter after the fall of King Olaf the Saint; and Snorri the Chieftain was buried at home there in Sælingsdalstunga, at the church he himself had had built there. He has been greatly blessed in his descendants, for most of the best-born men in Iceland trace their kin to him, as well as the men of Bjarkey in Halogaland and the Gata-folk in the Faroes, and many other great men, not mentioned here, both here in this country and in others. When . . .[2]

[1] Corrected from twenty.
[2] The text breaks off with this word.

A list of translations of Icelandic texts mentioned in the Notes

CHAPTER-NUMBERS in the translations may not always coincide with the references given in the notes. The latter are taken throughout from the editions published in the series *Íslenzk Fornrit* (Reykjavík, 1933–).

1. *Bjarnar saga Hítdœlakappa*.
   Not in English; in German in F. Niedner, *Vier Skalden-geschichten* (*Thule*, IX; Jena, 1914; new edition, 1922).

2. *Egils saga Skalla-Grímssonar*.
   (i) W. C. Green, *The Story of Egil Skallagrimsson*. London, 1893.
   (ii) E. R. Eddison, *Egil's Saga*. Cambridge, 1930.
   (iii) Gwyn Jones, *Egil's Saga*. Syracuse University Press, for the American-Scandinavian Foundation, 1960.
   (iv) Christine Fell, *Egils Saga*. London, 1975 (in Dent's Everyman's University Library, No. 251).
   (v) Hermann Pálsson and Paul Edwards, *Egil's Saga*. Penguin Books. London, 1976.

3. *Eiríks saga rauða*.
   (i) In A. M. Reeves, *The Finding of Wineland the Good*. London, 1890.
   (ii) In G. M. Gathorne-Hardy, *The Norse Discoverers of America*. Oxford, 1921.
   (iii) In Gwyn Jones, *Eirik the Red and other Icelandic Sagas*. Oxford University Press. The World's Classics, No. 582. London, 1961.

4. *Eyrbyggja saga*.
   (i) William Morris and Eiríkr Magnússon, *The Story of the Ere-Dwellers* (*The Saga Library*, II; London, 1892).
   (ii) P. Schach, *Eyrbyggja Saga*. University of Nebraska Press and the American-Scandinavian Foundation, 1959.

5. *Fóstbræðra saga.*

In Lee M. Hollander, *The Sagas of Kormák and the Sworn Brothers.* Princeton University Press for the American-Scandinavian Foundation, 1949.

6. *Grettis saga.*

(i) Eiríkr Magnússon and William Morris, *Grettis Saga: The Story of Grettir the Strong.* London, 1869 (first and second editions), 1901 (third edition).

(ii) G. A. Hight, *The Saga of Grettir the Strong.* London, 1914 (in Dent's Everyman's Library, No. 699).

7. *Hávarðar saga Ísfirðings.*

William Morris and Eiríkr Magnusson, *The Story of Howard the Halt* (*The Saga Library*, I; London, 1891).

8. *Heimskringla.*

(i) S. Laing, *The Heimskringla.* London, 1844 (first edition), 1889 (second edition); in Dent's Everyman's Library, No. 717 (*Heimskringla: The Olaf Sagas*; London, 1915), and No. 847 (*Heimskringla: The Norse King Sagas*; London, 1930, and in a revised edition, 1961).

(ii) William Morris and Eiríkr Magnússon, *The Stories of the Kings of Norway called The Round of World* (*Heimskringla*) (*The Saga Library*, III–VI; London, 1893–1905).

(iii) E. Monsen and A. H. Smith, *Heimskringla.* Cambridge, 1932.

9. *Hrafnkels saga.*

In Gwyn Jones, *Four Icelandic Sagas.* Princeton University Press, for the American-Scandinavian Foundation, 1935. And in Gwyn Jones, *Eirik the Red* (see No. 3 above).

10. *Hrafns saga Sveinbjarnarsonar.*

Anne Tjomsland, *The Saga of Hrafn Sveinbjarnarson* (*Islandica*, XXXV; Ithaca, New York, 1951).

11. *Íslendingabók.*

Halldór Hermannsson, *The Book of the Icelanders* (*Íslendingabók*) (*Islandica*, XX; Ithaca, New York, 1930).

12. *Kormáks saga.*

(i) W. G. Collingwood and Jón Stefánsson, *The Life and Death of Cormac the Skald* (*Viking Club Translation Series*, No. I; Ulverston, 1902).

(ii) In Lee M. Hollander, *The Sagas of Kormák and the Sworn Brothers* (see No. 5 above).

13. *Landnámabók*.

T. Ellwood, *The Book of the Settlement of Iceland*. Kendal, 1898.

14. *Laxdæla saga*.

(i) M. A. C. Press, *Laxdæla Saga*. London, 1899. In Dent's Everyman's Library (No. 597). London, 1964.

(ii) R. Proctor, *The Story of the Laxdalers*. London, 1903.

(iii) Thorstein Veblen, *The Laxdæla Saga*. New York, 1925.

15. *Njáls saga*.

(i) G. W. Dasent, *The Story of Burnt Njal*. Edinburgh, 1861 (first edition, in two volumes); London, 1900 (second edition, ed. E. V. Lucas); in Dent's Everyman's Library, No. 558; London, 1911 and 1956.

(ii) Magnus Magnusson and Hermann Pálsson, *Njal's Saga*. The Penguin Classics, 1960.

16. *Vatnsdæla saga*.

Gwyn Jones, *The Vatnsdalers' Saga*. Princeton University Press for the American-Scandinavian Foundation, 1944.

17. *Viga-Glúms saga*.

Sir Edmund Head, *Viga-Glum's Saga*. London, 1866.

Texts and translations (in whole or in part) of Nos. 11 and 13 are in Volume I and of Nos. 3–5, 7, 9, 12, 14, 16, 17 in Volume II of Gudbrand Vigfusson and F. York Powell, *Origines Islandicae*. Oxford, 1905.

An Essay on the Saga of Gisli and its Icelandic Background

I

THE FIRST permanent settlement in Iceland was made in or about the year 870. Contemporary events in English affairs were the martyrdom of Edmund, King of the East Angles, in 870, and Alfred's succession to the throne of Wessex, in 871. The first settler in Iceland was a well-born Norwegian, Ingolf Arnarson, who took into possession a large tract of land in the south-west and built his homestead at Reykjavík—the site of the modern capital. Many other men followed his example and within the following sixty years all the land in Iceland had been taken into possession. The settlers were mainly from the west and south-west of Norway. A fair proportion, however, perhaps about one in eight, either came from Norwegian families living in the Celtic parts of the British Isles (Orkney, Scotland, Hebrides, Man and Ireland, where invasion and settlement had gone on since at least the beginning of the ninth century), or else had themselves so-journed for some time in those parts. They brought with them slaves of Celtic stock, and some of the Norwegian families had Celtic blood in them.

It is said that the first settlers found Irish hermits already living in Iceland, and that these left on the arrival of the Norse-men. Apart from these, Iceland had had no previous inhabitants.

Conditions of life were relatively easy, chiefly because of the unspoilt bird- and seal-hunting and the rich fisheries. There was much woodland, although it could not have provided much timber of any size, and excellent grazing. On the great estates the settlers established themselves in a farming life in the style they had been accustomed to in Norway and the British Isles. The emphasis lay on the cultivation of corn and grass and the pasturing of cattle and sheep for meat and dairy produce. As time went on corn-growing became less and less important and finally disappeared completely in the sixteenth century.

Little could be expected in the way of social organization amongst men of different local origins, arriving in small groups in a new country and at intervals spread over a long period. Bonds of kinship, where they existed, must have been a great source of strength in such a community, and they seem to have been carefully fostered in the new surroundings. In general it seems that the head of a family, having been captain of the ship or ships that brought him and his household, now became squire and master in his own 'land-taking'. The pattern was developed and modified as soon as he began to distribute land amongst his sons and followers, and a man's position as a leader naturally depended on his willingness to exert authority and the willingness of those who lived round him to accept it. That there were many local shifts, rebellions and feuds in the early period is suggested by some of the anecdotes told in the *Book of the Settlements* (*Landnámabók*), our chief source concerning the origins of the Icelandic Commonwealth. In the first half-century of the Settlement, however, the mere sharing in the struggle against difficulties common to all must have largely contributed to a general sense of communal identity: the inhabitants had become Icelanders. By the end of that time conditions were stable enough for a general system of local authority to exist. The *thing*, a public assembly for deliberation and decision attended by all the freemen of the tribe, is an ancient feature of Germanic social organization, and this type of assembly was established in Iceland, as elsewhere in Scandinavian settlements abroad. We have certain information about only one such *thing* in Iceland before about 930. This was established at Kjalarnes by the son of Ingolf, the first settler, whose family continued to enjoy prestige on his account throughout the Commonwealth period. There were doubtless others elsewhere in the country, although they would not be looked on with such respect nor perhaps show the same degree of formal organization as the one at Kjalarnes.

In connection with the *thing*-organization there developed a generally accepted oligarchical system of local and national 'government'. This development depended on and was influenced by a number of factors: the varied origin of the settlers and the different kinds of customary law they were used to; the conditions of the settlement; the prestige and solidarity of important families; the delicate position of the chieftain with inherited or self-made authority in a society where freedom and free speech in public affairs were the valued birthright of the majority, whatever their standing or wealth. Under the circumstances, a co-operative solution was inevitable, autocracy impossible.

What happened was that, about the year 920, it was decided to create a code of law and a general *thing* for the whole nation. The decision was apparently taken on the initiative of the chief men in the south-west, with Ingolf's family at their head. A learned man called Ulfljot was then sent to Norway, with the task of adapting to Icelandic conditions the laws of the Gulathing—the code, itself only recently standardized, that applied in the Norwegian districts from which most of the settlers had come. Meanwhile a site for a national assembly, the *Althing*, was selected, the magnificent *Þingvöllr* at the head of the great lake called *Ölfusvatn*, just outside the borders of Ingolf's land, some thirty miles from Reykjavík. On Ulfljot's return the first assembly was held there (*c.* 925) and his code of law adopted for the whole country. By this a constitutional system was established in which the essential power lay in the hands of the *godar* (sing. *godi*), the local leaders, of whom there were probably thirty-six at this time. These leaders deliberated and voted in that part of the *Althing* called the Legislative Court and they nominated judges to act in the Judicial Court. As president of the whole assembly a Law-Speaker was elected by the *godar*, for a term of three years in the first instance. It was the Law-Speaker's duty to know the whole law (it was taught by word of mouth and learnt by heart), to recite one-third of the code each summer at the *Althing*, and to impart the law on specific matters to any inquirer; he sat as chairman of the Legislative Court and was the only paid servant of the Commonwealth.

On a national scale the balance of power seems to have been well ensured, partly by the comparatively large number of *godar*, who in political and social status were more or less equal and

95

whose way of life could not differ much from that of any reasonably well-to-do farmer, and partly by the peculiar nature of the authority, or *godord*, which each held. The power of a *godi* depended in the last resort on the number and quality of his *thingmen*. Every freeman had by law to be 'in thing with' some leader, but originally there were no rules as to which. The relationship between *godi* and *thingman* was technically a personal bond between the two, a contract for mutual aid and support which was freely entered upon and which could be renounced at will. As a result the authority of a leader had no territorial limits, and a man might choose to support and be supported by some *godi* in a different district from the one he lived in himself. One may, of course, wonder how far an energetic chieftain would allow any man in his immediate vicinity to owe allegiance to anyone but himself. To keep his following the *godi* had to deal justly and generously with his *thingmen*, when they had disputes amongst themselves or were in trouble; externally he could offer them energetic leadership and support, especially in legal disputes. It is obvious, however, that the number and quality of his *thingmen* could serve as much to restrain as to encourage an aggressive chieftain. The *godord* itself was also regarded in a way that made tyranny difficult: it was authority, an asset conceived in a way somewhat similar to the 'goodwill' of a modern business concern; it could be bought and sold, lent, inherited and shared or held in turn by members of a family.

We know little about the organization of local assemblies in the first part of the tenth century. About 960, however—near the time when Gisli was outlawed—the organization was reformed and we know the system that obtained from then onward. The country was then divided into four Quarters, denoted by the cardinal compass points, and in each Quarter there were three '*thing*-districts', save in the Northern Quarter where, because of a local quarrel, they had to have four. A '*thing*-district' covered the main 'territory' of three *godar* (who were now not allowed to have *thingmen* outside their own Quarter), and in each district a specific named place was now appointed or confirmed as the local assembly-site. Thorsness and Thorskafjord *things*, which figure in the story of Gisli, were such assembly-places. The principal local meeting was the spring-*thing*, where local affairs were discussed under the leadership of the *godar*, and where legal cases were heard before judges, appointed, as at the *Althing*, by the chieftains. Widespread knowledge of the law and widespread active participation in legal procedure must have been a stabilizing social influence in its encouragement of respect for law and legal form.

The settlers in Iceland were mostly heathen, whose religious life centred on social cult acts of propitiatory sacrifice. The chief objects of public cults were the gods Thor and Frey, the latter, as appears also in the story of Gisli, particularly a god of fertility. (Odin was not, in Iceland, and hardly in Norway, a 'social' god in the same sense—he appears as the patron of individuals, but his sanctuary was the battlefield and the slain his sacrifice.) The chieftain derives his title *godi* (from the word 'god') from his function as priestly leader of the sacrifices organized for the public good. It was his responsibility to maintain the local temple, to which a temple-tax was paid, although we do not know what this amounted to or whether it made any significant difference to the *godi*'s income. The organization of the *things* and the legal system they represented were closely linked with the heathen faith: each *thing* was 'hallowed' before it began by one of the *godar*—at the *Althing* the ceremony was performed by the holder of the *godord* of Ingolf's family, whose importance was thus recognized—and oaths, which played an important part in legal procedure, were sworn by invoking the names of certain gods.

A few important settlers are known, however, to have been Christian or at least mixed in their beliefs. Doubtless most of the Celtic slaves and dependants were Christian too, but there is no way of knowing what kind of leavening these may have produced in the predominantly Norse population. Some acquaintance with Christianity must have been widespread throughout the tenth century, inherited or acquired through journeys abroad. Attempts to convert the Icelanders to Christianity began about 980, and finally, in the year 1000, under strong pressure from the missionary king of Norway, Olaf Tryggvason, the *Althing* accepted Christianity as the faith of the nation. This decision could not be taken without compromise between the heathen and Christian parties, and for some years, at any rate, the law permitted the zealous pagan to go on sacrificing in secret. There was of course a large formal element in the Conversion: the cult-act was changed but the community expected at least the same public benefits from the new God as they had done from the old gods. But in the compromise between pagan and Christian apparent in the *Althing*'s decision we find a typical sign of a deep-rooted mental attitude in the Icelanders—an attitude which played no small part in their preservation of a great wealth of pre-Christian poetry and mythological lore and in their creation of the classical saga-literature of the thirteenth century.

The two centuries after the Conversion were by and large a period of peaceful and fruitful development in society and Church. By about 1100 economic developments and the disappearance of slavery as an institution had brought about the virtual elimination of the very great estates and the emergence of a large class of reasonably prosperous freemen-farmers. We do not know of any great political troubles in this period, and the influence of the Church was growing stronger. The first native bishop was consecrated in 1056; the country was divided into two dioceses in 1106; the first monastery, a Benedictine foundation, was established in 1133. Relations between prominent families and the Church were necessarily close, because the church buildings belonged to the farmers on whose land they stood and it was the farmers who employed the priests to serve them. Many members of good families took orders—sometimes, doubtless, merely to keep the church and all its income within the family. It was most important of all, however, that such men came through the Church into contact with established forms of intellectual activity, chiefly theology and history but also music and mathematics, which stimulated them and which they in turn fostered. The significant cultural contribution of medieval Iceland is a specifically literary one, and its major source lies in the unique blend of pagan inheritance and Christian acquisition which belongs to this period.

By the end of the twelfth century several political and family disputes show the signs of a new age. Soon after 1200 there were widespread feuds between chieftains, sometimes involving important churchmen as well. The metropolitan see of Nidaros in Norway was not satisfied with the state of the Church in Iceland, in which the secular hand played too large a part; and the King of Norway was disposed to regard a headless state like Iceland as an absurdity, just as everyone else in Europe would have done, had they known about it. The policy of bringing Iceland under the Norwegian Crown was aided by circumstances, although it took time to accomplish. The Icelanders' commercial dependence on their Norwegian connections was a useful weapon in the king's hands. Relations between Crown and Church in Norway were often such as to ensure sympathetic ecclesiastical instruments for the prosecution of royal policy. Continuing disputes in Iceland, chief against chief and chief against bishop, brought many complainants to the king's court, asking his help to gain redress or restoration. In such cases the situation was bedevilled by the confused loyalties which resulted from the old custom of making Icelanders members of the royal retinue: the king usually derived advantage from this, for it was a time when the personal bond of loyalty to liege lord was stronger than most other ties. For about forty years the pressure continued, a period of political unrest and bitter feud, until in 1262–4 the Icelanders agreed to pay tribute to the Norwegian Crown. They were supposed to keep their old institutions, but the *godord* authority had partly disappeared in the troublous times and it now went for good. The old native law-code, which doubtless needed reform, was replaced by recent Norwegian codes imperfectly adapted to Icelandic conditions, and by the end of the century a new internal organization was being introduced, based on the sheriff with his allotted territory to administer or exploit. By this time, too, the Church in Iceland, after a long struggle, had achieved its aims in matters relating to the ownership and administration of churches and property donated to them. Its servants, as members of a state within a state, were free to pursue wealth, power, learning and the arts, as well as the contemplative life and the cure of souls. Although the division between secular and ecclesiastic now appears marked in comparison with the early period, it was never as far-reaching as in most west European countries. Education was primarily the Church's work, and in the fourteenth century it appears to have been of the same standard as before and equally widespread. In the twelfth century the tools and methods which the education of the Church had put into men's hands were actively applied to their native inheritance, pagan and early Christian, especially in the fields of history and poetry. In the fourteenth century the Icelanders had literary resources in abundance and those that meant most to them were the great secular works, the Kings' Sagas and the Sagas of Icelanders, written in the intervening period. Few original works of this kind were written in the fourteenth century, but the many copies, the great compilations and the splendid codices of the period testify to the enduring popularity of the older vernacular literature.

2

THE ICELANDERS must have begun to write their native language, using forms of Latin script which the Church taught them, in the course of the eleventh century. The first written works were undoubtedly set down in order to serve the Church's aims of education and edification—sermons, translated or original, must have been especially important. The first secular literary works date from the second and third decade of the twelfth century. The work of codifying in book form the laws of the country began in 1117; and soon after 1120 Ari Thorgilsson the Learned wrote a short history of the Icelandic people. (The oldest extant fragment of a legal code dates from *c.* 1150; Ari's work is known only in two seventeenth-century transcripts of an original that must have been written about 1200.) In the course of the twelfth century a large number of learned men, clerical and lay, fostered a zealous antiquarian interest. Despite the eagerness with which they appear to have sought and recorded all kinds of historical information, they were often by no means devoid of a critical attitude towards their sources. The great monument of their work, which must be regarded as the result of co-operative effort, is the *Book of the Settlements* (*Landnámabók*), in which details of the family and 'land-taking' of over four hundred of the first settlers are given. Another example of their work is the so-called *Ævi Snorra goða* (*Life of Snorri the Chieftain*), a brief biographical sketch, now fragmentary, of a single great leader in the years round 1000 (see p. 88). This record is of some importance for the study of the saga of Gisli, and it will be mentioned again below.

The interest of the Icelandic antiquarians and historians was not confined to their own country. In varying forms it took in most of Scandinavia and the world of Scandinavian expansion. Above all it turned to Norway, the country from which their ancestors had come, whose kings had been largely influential in converting Iceland to Christianity, the place where many Icelanders still sought service, profit and advancement, and where they felt at home. Sæmund Sigfusson, an older contemporary of Ari Thorgilsson, wrote a Latin work on the history of the kings of Norway, and Ari included information about their reigns in the first edition of his history of the Icelanders—both of these works are unfortunately lost. Just after the middle of the twelfth century an Icelander called Eirik Oddsson composed a history of the contemporary Norwegian kings, and thereafter an unbroken series of Kings' Sagas was produced, many of them now known to us in different versions and embodied in different compilations. The last to be written was a life of King Magnus the Law-mender, who died in 1280. The most famous of these histories— and deservedly so—is Snorri Sturluson's *Heimskringla*, written *c*. 1223–35, which covers the reigns of the kings of Norway from the half-legendary age preceding the unification of the kingdom *c*. 900 down to 1177.

It cannot be said that the sort of history cultivated in the earlier part of the twelfth century lent itself to the development of narrative prose of high quality. By the beginning of the thirteenth century, however, more than one master of vivid and supple prose had emerged, notably the unknown authors of some of the oldest *þættir*, or short stories, found in the earliest collections of Kings' Sagas, and Karl Jonsson, abbot of the Benedictine house at Þingeyrar, author of part or all of the *Sverris saga*, a history of the reign of King Sverrir of Norway (1181–1202). And after the limpid narrative, sober pragmatism and conscious artistry of Snorri Sturluson, certain virtues of style seem almost to have become innate in the authors of the sagas.

Fundamental to the study of the past in early Iceland was the study of poetry. The most common activity of the poet in ancient Scandinavia was eulogy of king or lord, and famous examples of this kind must have been used to school the young poet. In the twelfth and thirteenth centuries Icelandic historians could seek material for their narrative in such poems, many of which were, after all, sources more or less contemporary with the events they describe. Icelanders had capacious memories for verse telling of kings and battles, and there was also much verse of a more domestic kind that was eagerly remembered. Many Icelanders were poets, and linked with their adventures were verses, one or more, which served as the kernel or ornament of anecdotes about them. Many such verses are now preserved in the Sagas of Ice-landers. The art of scaldic poetry depends for the most part on highly wrought diction and highly wrought metres (cf. pp. 61-3), and the intricacy of the form must have played an important part in making their accurate preservation possible. But the problem of deciding whether a given verse is authentic or not is extremely complex and difficult. Some of the reasons why this is so will be considered later in the discussion of the verse in the saga of Gisli.

The first sagas of Icelanders were probably composed about the end of the twelfth century. Their principal subjects are the exploits and careers of men and women who lived, broadly speaking, between the end of the Settlement Period, *c.* 930, and the first Christian generation, *c.* 1030. The central figures in the narrative are real: information about them had been preserved most effectively by the genealogical and antiquarian zeal of the preceding period, and it is noteworthy that the heroes of most of the earliest sagas were well-known 'court-poets' and that much verse attributed to them was used and quoted in their stories. Many of the events described in the sagas undoubtedly took place and had been remembered, more or less accurately, in a man's family or locality; some tangible reminder, a verse, a place, a place name, an heirloom, might serve to keep the memory alive through generations. But many of the things reported as fact cannot be controlled in any way, and while we may reasonably give credence to a central fact, that Gisli killed Thorgrim, for example, we have no means of establishing the veracity of the saga's account of the circumstances under which such an event took place. Critical study of a number of sagas has shown either that the major characters could not have done what is ascribed to them or that they could not have done it in the way described. These works are thus a mixture of history and imagination, the interests of the author and the material at his disposal conditioning his preference for or need of the one or other element, not always in the same measure in different parts of his story and not always without conflict between the two. In general it may be said that the authors of these sagas possessed enough historical imagination and enough authentic information, both of a general and particular kind, to avoid gross errors and anachronisms in their presentation of men and women who had lived two or three hundred years before them. It need perhaps hardly be said that the age in which the sagas were composed saw nothing unreal in stories of ghosts and omens and dreams.

The composition of such sagas was continued and developed throughout the thirteenth century, The earliest known stories of this kind, from *c.* 1200, *Heiðarvíga saga*, *Kormáks saga*, *Fóst-bræðra saga*, show deficiencies in style and construction compared with the later well-organized and smoothly flowing texts. When we remember the evidence available of contemporary skill in the handling of narrative prose, such faults cannot be taken as evidence of a general primitive stage in the development of Icelandic letters. They must mean, however, that in this particular kind of saga standards of taste and narrative conventions were still not wholly established. By about 1240 a number of other important and influential works of this type had been written, including the *Hallfreðar saga*, *Bjarnar saga Hítdœlakappa* and *Droplaugarsona saga*, as well as the great *Egils saga Skalla-Grímssonar*, which in many respects stands apart from all other sagas and is the first of them on the scale of a full-length novel.

With these works and others from about the middle of the century the 'classical' saga acquired its specific form. Different though they are in subject and treatment, and impossible though it is to point to any single saga as a flawless example of the ideal, there are certain major features common to them all in greater or less degree, and these may be isolated and regarded as essential.

There is first a basic community of outlook in the saga-writers. They were dealing with pre-Christian men and women, as they knew full well, and it suited neither their philosophy nor their prejudices to make their characters mentally and morally subject to the heathen pantheon. The gods might be held responsible for a man's good or bad fortune, but they had nothing to do with his character—and it is the individual human character in which the writers were most deeply interested. A code of conduct must exist, however, and the writers endowed their characters with a heroic outlook: they saw them ultimately at the mercy of an inexorable fate and interpreted their careers as examples of courage and defiance in the face of the misfortune and death that fate brought upon them. There is no doubt that this heroic outlook also answered to the personal ideals of many men in the thirteenth century itself. It was a time of strife and conflicting loyalties, when men often had to make a hard choice and were brought face to face with stark chance, when courage was almost the only thing to fall back on. This recrudescence of the heroic mentality must have encouraged the outlook expressed in the sagas; and the cleanliness of the ideals expressed in the sagas must in turn have helped to foster a like response in the men who heard and read them.

The driving force throughout was the need to maintain the integrity and honour of oneself and one's family, and to this end the public vindication of reputation was essential. When the Icelandic constitution was evolved in the tenth century provisions for the execution of judgments made in the courts were willingly left inadequate: punishment and redress were in the end the business of the individual, aided though he might be by public opinion and the local chiefs. The paramount duty remained the duty of vengeance, when justice was done and, equally important from the point of view of a man's good name, seen to be done. Vengeance was sanctioned most fully against a man who had been outlawed by the courts, but in many cases feuds never got to the *thing*, or reached no conclusion there if they did, and the system was worked out in private. The sagas are alive with a passion for justice of this kind, but they also reveal a nobler appreciation of the beauty of conduct—which is their fundamental preoccupation. The greatest admiration, apart from that reserved for the brave man meeting danger and death with equanimity, is given to a quality called *drengskapr*, a difficult word to translate. It implies the opposite of all meanness of spirit and action: the quality of a man who lays down his life for his friend, who takes no advantage of an unarmed or sleeping enemy, who in the midst of a family feud can admire not hate his adversary. At its best it implies the highest standards of fair play, touched by a certain magnanimity and even graciousness of mind. Expression of this ideal may at times become little more than conventional, but a real regard for it continually appears in the sagas of Icelanders, where it often brings light into what might otherwise merely be a sombre succession of vengeful deeds.

The outlook of the saga-writers is imbued with a humanism which is at once deep and expansive and narrow and stern. Their characters are not limited to any one social class, and all sorts of men and women may play a significant part in the action. The authors show immense skill in individualizing their chief men and women—they are rarely puppets or types. On the other hand they usually study their characters as they are, rarely showing them in development, as characters who become better or worse in some way. And they apply one standard to all: they approve when a man, slave or freeman or noble behaves like a man; they have no sympathy when he fails to do this, however much such failure might be attributed to external or involuntary causes. In the story of Gisli we have an intentional parallelism between two episodes which illustrates this point, the one concerning the character and fate of the bondservant, Thord the coward, the other the character and fate of the bondwoman, Bothild (chs. 13, 20, 26–7). Thord is a coward, he is useless; Gisli saves his own life by using Thord as a decoy, and Thord is killed—it does not matter. Bothild helps Gisli to escape as well, but she does it in a brave, active, positive way: she is rewarded with her freedom. Everywhere we find the same essential respect for the boundless freedom and power of the individual human will.

Although the writers are thus preoccupied with human character, they do not concern themselves directly with the thoughts and emotions of their people, but only with the speech and action that spring from them. They describe conduct in order to reveal character. There is no playing on the feelings, no dwelling on pleasure or pain at any time; and although men's actions may be fierce and ruthless, there is little or no cruelty or torture in the sagas.

This objectivity of approach is reflected in their narrative technique. The writer appears to be detached from his story; he rarely intrudes his own views, except sometimes by quoting the 'voice of the countryside', when the opinion expressed becomes part of the story and is not felt as an intrusion at all. The sagas are in the form of the novel, mixed narrative and dialogue, but they also accept some of the chief limitations of the drama: thoughts and emotions must be physically perceived, heard or seen in speech and action. This visual technique is often applied even in open-air action, in a way reminiscent of the film, when we are first presented with an unidentified picture at long range, a picture which is not identified until the range is short enough to make it clear. The author, it may be said, does his best to mingle with the participants in the events described, to be an impartial spectator of the drama which is being played out for the first time, as it were, not merely revived for the reader's benefit. In general, he wishes only to describe what it was possible for a spectator to know: the monologue was inadmissible and private conversation restricted. (In the saga of Gisli however there is much intimate talk, and this helps to give the story its peculiar frankness of tone.) Such an objective approach demands a highly developed sense of proportion controlling the selection of material. It is sometimes surprising how far ahead a writer looks in introducing what seems at first sight an insignificant detail. In ch. 15 of the saga of Gisli we are told that the floors at Saebol were strewn with rushes from the rush-pond. If we notice this at all, we probably think of it only as a rudimentary piece of interior description. It is only later, in ch. 16, that we see that it has a point in the development of the action itself, for it is with twists made from these rushes on the floor that Gisli puts out the lights in the sleeping-room before attacking Thorgrim.

The style of the classical sagas is sober and pragmatic; it avoids all kinds of exuberance and leaves much to the intelligent inference of the reader. A brilliant example of the effects that can be achieved by the conventional restraint and reticence of the sagas is found in the few lines describing Gislis's approach to the bedside of his sister and brother-in-law and his stabbing of Thorgrim in ch. 16. The author becomes Gisli at this point, sees with his eyes, feels with his hands. It is well worth considering how much he does not tell us and how easy it would be for any modern author to write up such an account.[1] In the saga there is here a supremely effective balance between the relentless intensity of the terse, taut narrative, with its occasional vivid and telling detail, and the cool, even tone of the refined colloquial language in which it is conveyed.

3

THE SAGA OF Gisli can be appreciated at various levels. In many ways it corresponds to the usual type of Icelandic saga in background and incident and style. But it stands apart from all other stories of this class in its essential theme and the author's treatment of it. In the sagas generally honour is the emphatic keynote. Love between man and woman is not infrequently the source of action, but its implications are not deeply explored. In the saga of Gisli, however, we find interplay and open conflict between personal and family honour and personal and family love—the relationships could hardly be more complex, between brother and

---

[1] Or indeed any ancient writer. There is for example, an early Icelandic translation of St Jerome's life of St Paul of Thebes, with its vivid account of Antonius's arrival at the hermit's cave: 'Antonius goes in nevertheless, despite the dark, to find out what was going on, and makes his way as silently as he can, acts with much cunning, draws his breath softly, stops now and then and listens about to catch any sound.' (This from the Icelandic; cf. the Latin: '. . . suspenso gradu, et anhelitu temperato, callidus explorator ingressus: ac paulatim progrediens, sæpiusque subsistens, sonum aure captabat.') It is clear that the Icelanders chose to write as they did; it was not because they were incapable or ignorant of anything else.

brother, brother and sister, man and wife, as well as between friends and blood-brothers—while both honour and love are looked upon as equally powerful, though not always as equally justifiable, motives for action. The result is a sustained dramatic sequence of highly charged emotional relationships between the central characters, expressed in much less restrained terms than is usual in other sagas. The dominant theme is found at the outset of the narrative, in the Norwegian prehistory of Gisli and his family. The importance of this prelude lies almost entirely in its definition of the central characters, Gisli himself, his brother Thorkell and sister Thordis. Gisli is honourable, strict and ruthless; Thorkell is weaker, although the elder of the two; he is on affectionate terms with his sister, whose suitors he aids, even though it is against the honour of the family; he seeks his friends outside his own family; Thordis is 'handsome and intelligent', willing to be wooed. By the time they leave Norway, Thorkell has lost two men he had made his friends, killed by Gisli, and Thordis has lost three suitors. This should never be forgotten in the course of the rest of the story, where the essential action springs from the same or similar emotional relationships and crises.

The writer was well aware of the ugliness of tormented feeling, and he is willing to convey the pain and pettiness of it. In the scene after the death of Vestein (ch. 14), Thorkell twice asks Gisli how Aud, the dead man's sister and Gisli's wife, bore her loss. The reason for this reiterated question is not perhaps immediately clear, but the author's intention is revealed when one recalls the conversation between Aud and Asgerd, which Thorkell overheard (ch. 9). In that conversation he learnt of his wife's preference for Vestein, but it was in Aud's last words there—'I have had nothing to do with a man since I married Gisli'—that the intolerable innuendo lay—that Asgerd, his wife, had had something to do with Vestein since their marriage. Thorkell now responds in character: he wants Aud to be hurt at her brother's death, and he wants to know she is hurt. While the author of the story of Gisli may not have had a deeper insight into the human mind than other saga-writers, he was willing to probe into darker and remoter corners of it than they.

One expects to find skill in character portrayal in an Icelandic saga, and in the story of Gisli it is there in full measure. Apart from Gisli and Aud, it is Thorkell and Thordis who make most impression. Thorkell has a consistently conveyed character—he is vain, ineffectual, resentful, an aristocratic disposition with its virtues stunted by self-pity. Good and bad are mixed in him in natural human measure. We recognize him but we do not respect him. In him, and more especially in Thordis, there is a suggestion of complexity which is denied Gisli and Aud themselves. Thordis is the most interesting of all. She is presented in the normal restrained way of the Icelandic saga, but the author sees to it that there are enough hints to lead our imaginations in the right direction. She is the only character in the story who finds himself or herself in a truly tragic situation, when she has to choose between husband and brother. Led by love for her dead husband and, one feels, by resentment that Gisli should have put his wife's brother before his sister's husband, she chooses husband and betrays Gisli's secret. Gisli's verse, 'Wife-veil-hearted wavering' (ch. 19), pointedly contrasts her action with the Gudrun of heroic legend, who when her brothers took her husband's life sought no vengeance on them, but when her second husband killed her brothers took a most terrible vengeance on him. But Thordis has a high integrity all the same—she sets her own standards and solves her own problems. There is nothing out of keeping when at the end she makes a spirited attack on Eyjolf, Gisli's slayer, and divorces herself from Bork, despite the fact that they have only executed the man whom she herself had condemned. It is typical of the irony and constant parallelism of the story's presentation that Gisli ultimately also finds himself in a position where he must choose between wife and brother—when Thorkell is killed by Aud's nephews, sons of Vestein: he chooses his wife.

Gisli appears as the typical hero, a man of many parts, a fighter at once bold and resourceful and ruthless, good with his hands, a loyal friend, punctilious in matters of honour. He zealously upholds the good name and solidarity of his family, and it is an essential part of his tragedy that he expects his brother and sister to do the same and cannot understand them when they do not. It is a weakness in the story that the author expends little care on the characters of Bork and Eyjolf, Gisli's chief antagonists. They are little more than caricatures, and with such foils as these the hero's own stature is ultimately diminished. In other ways, however, Gisli's character is presented in by no means typical fashion. His devotion to his wife is expressed with the uncommon frankness of this author, and it is a feeling which plays its part as a motive for action in the narrative. Gisli himself is not free from self-pity—it is most apparent in his meetings with Thorkell, his brother (chs. 23 and 24). He is also supposed to have been a poet and a dreamer, and in the verses which convey his dreams are laid bare the sensibilities of a man tormented by anxiety about a life after death—not otherwise a preoccupation that saga-writers attributed to their heroes. He has two dream women, the one brings him hope, the other despair; his end is presaged by a stream of verses in which the repeated symbol is that of blood; a less unusual sequence of verses reveals the dream-omens of the last battle he is to fight. It was a bold attempt on the author's part to combine these dual aspects in the single character, but not a wholly successful one. The chief impression that remains of Gisli is that he is essentially a simplex character, truly at home in the wholesome adventure stuff of most of the narrative. The dream-woman symbolism, with its notes of the sentimental and pathetic, is in strange contrast and, while it adds variety to his character, it adds little depth. This impression is no doubt partly due to the facile quality of much of the verse and its symbolism. Two explanations are offered by the prose for this duality. On the one hand it is implied that he came under Christian influence in Viborg, which caused him to stop sacrificing, and that it is a sort of crisis in religious faith which he is undergoing in his dreams. On the other hand it is suggested that Gisli's disturbed mind and general restlessness while outlawed are due to the effects of black magic. The latter explanation is of a common type, often resorted to in the sagas to make the unaccountable plausible. The former is undoubtedly in better accord with the verses, where the two dream women can be interpreted as figures related to the good and bad angels who struggle over a man's soul—a common medieval theme. Yet it is difficult to see how much weight the author of the saga himself attached to this idea. The poet of the dream-verses appears to have had the idea of internal religious conflict much more clearly (cf. pp. 119–23 below).

Whatever the reader's response to the peculiar emotional emphasis in the saga and the complication of character caused by the introduction of the dreams and their symbolism, there is much in the style and construction of the story to which all will accord the highest praise. The author achieves a masterly tension in the description of the efforts to warn Vestein not to come to Saebol and in the stylized series of premonitions of disaster that he meets on his journey, as well as in the description of the death of Vestein and of Thorgrim; and there is a graphic excitement in the stories of Gisli's tight corners and escapes. In such passages one is willing to overlook some inconsistencies: the fact, for example, that the recognition of Vestein by Geirmund and Rannveig and what follows from it is superfluous, just as later on Gisli ties sixty cows' tails together for no practical purpose whatever. In this latter case, as in the story of Gisli's hiding in the bed of Ref's termagant wife and the story of the dispersal of the cairn, the writer is using a stock situation, which he presents with great skill but not always so adapted as to achieve total consistency. This is a not uncommon feature of saga-narrative, however, and two considerations are relevant to its appreciation. It is possible, on the one hand, that common contemporary knowledge (whether historically true or false) may have required the inclusion in a given story of intransigent material; and on the other hand it must be recalled that, although the saga of Gisli we have was written or dictated by its author, it was composed in what was largely an 'oral' world, where the common means of communication were through tongue and ear, not hand and eye, and where inevitably the part might well, and often safely, receive attention at some expense to the whole. But in general the author of the saga of Gisli strikes few false notes of this kind, and if he is on occasion brought perilously near the verge of the theatrically exaggerated, it is chiefly due to his taste for the emotional and pathetic. He appears to let his heart get the better of his head, for example, even in that famous episode where Ingjald helps Gisli to escape from Bork (ch. 26). The introductory conversation here is perhaps the most stilted in the whole saga, and Ingjald's reply to Bork's threats—'My clothes are threadbare, and it will not grieve me not to make them more so',—proud and affecting as it seems, has 'social' implications which will hardly stand critical reflection. It is part of the saga's realism to keep the characters this side of the abstract heroic—Gisli kills Bard without warning, for example, in ch. 2, and sacrifices Thord in ch. 20—but Ingjald is an exception. The result is close to heroics. The author may have had some inkling of this, for the Ingjald episode is followed almost immediately by the Ref episode, in which Gisli again escapes, but this time by hiding in the bed of Ref's wife, while she distracts Bork's men, who are searching the house, by pouring abuse on them. It is in burlesque contrast to the high seriousness which the author has attempted in the Ingjald episode, but Ref is just as effective in saving Gisli's life. Of course both Ingjald and Ref are cipher-characters, but in the context of the story Ref almost seems the easier to accept.

The formal construction of the saga is extraordinarily neat and effective. It divides essentially into two halves, each 'styled' in its own way. After the Norwegian prehistory, whose importance on one level has been suggested earlier, the story moves inexorably to the secret slayings of Vestein and Thorgrim. A succession of attempts to prevent the unknown but foreseeable disaster is brought to nothing—accidents, certainly regarded as tricks of fate, and the natural temperaments of the characters ensure that they are of no avail. It is in the nature of things, too, that failure in these attempts does not simply mean that the progression rests: each failure is itself a further step towards the end that is in fearful prospect. At the end of such episodes the voice of Gisli is heard, resignedly referring to the inescapable destiny; and there are many other notes of premonition. This is a story of deep and intricate emotional bonds, patterned against a background of ironic inevitability. The most distinctive feature of the presentation is its conscious parallelism, most obvious in the double secret slayings and the circumstances—the burial, the games—that follow them, but to be found elsewhere as well. Finally there comes the disclosure, when Gisli in an intentionally obscure verse reveals himself as Thorgrim's slayer. Thordis, Gisli's sister and Thorgrim's widow, hears and unravels the verse, and after some months she reveals it to Bork, her new husband, Thorgrim's brother, in a scene where the economical narrative is still adequate to suggest something of the intensity of her feeling. Thereafter Gisli's sentence and the first six years of his outlawry are passed over quickly, and we come to the second half of the story.

In this an account of the seven latter years of Gisli's outlawry is given, with the death of his brother Thorkell as the one decisive episode before the climax, Gisli's own death, is reached. The story is concluded in a chapter where the author dispenses neat justice and accounts for everyone else. This part does not have the same organic unity as the first half of the saga, but interest is maintained by the alternation of episodes where Gisli is seen outwitting his enemies and escaping their clutches and passages that describe his dreams and the suffering they cause him. In situations of the former kind the family emphasis is mainly on Gisli's relations with his brother Thorkell; in those of the latter kind, on his relations with his wife Aud. The writer's psychological insight and his preoccupation with the inner emotional life of his central characters are still allowed scope, but the episodic adventures of battle and escape, told with great spirit and ability, necessarily bring relief from the somewhat morbid and sentimental treatment of Gisli alone. The author aims at and achieves a cumulative effect in his descriptions of Gisli's dreams, which grow worse as his foretold days draw to their end, so that we have a moving impression that, when the time comes, Gisli is glad to have the action of his last fight and his death, as though this peace were welcome. The author is, I think, unique among saga-writers in trying to convey such a sense of inner exhaustion. Gisli's courage does not fail him, but there is something self-resigning and passive in the way he faces the hopelessness, very different from the defiant courage of the doomed heroes we meet in Germanic lay and epic and in other sagas of Icelanders. Neither can it be said that the writer has entirely succeeded in marrying this one strain in his narrative to the other strain, that of external action. The dreams and their sequence carry us on to the end, but, although we are told now and then that Gisli feels his enemies' net closing in around him, the threat from them does not appear to become more real and more urgent as the different episodes of pursuit, attack and escape are related. There is no progression in them—their number could be increased, their order altered, with small effect on the whole.

4

THE SAGA OF Gisli is a work of art written centuries ago and in a civilization different from our own. We shall never penetrate the essential mystery of its creation. We can, however, see some of the materials the author had to work on, and we can put the author and his book in a known Icelandic background, within limits of time and place.

The material of the story has diverse origins. Gisli and most of the other prominent characters were real men and women of the tenth century, and such things as the slayings of Vestein and Thorgrim, Gisli's outlawry, Thordis's marriages, are historical facts. A story like that of Thorgrim's slaying of the Norwegian merchants, one of the few extraneous pieces in the saga, is connected with the explanation of place names. Stock incidents have already been mentioned, for which no precise source need be sought, but in the description of Gisli's murder of Thorgrim we see the influence of a known piece of literature. The Norwegian place names in the opening part appear to be authentic and, with other elements, may perhaps depend on ancient reminiscence, as must also the author's knowledge of old burial customs, for example. The Icelandic topography is in general precisely and accurately described and must depend on the author's personal knowledge. There may well have been local and family traditions for the author to draw on, but it is clearly hard for us to distinguish between what may be due to these and what to the imagination and inventiveness of the author. There is finally the verse quoted in the story and all the background of ideas reflected in it. The verse poses fundamental problems and must be considered in some detail.

The study of scaldic verse is beset with many difficulties. Its metre is complex, its word-order free, its diction and imagery often obscure. There are often textual uncertainties. Once a small error is introduced in the written reproduction of such complex verse its interpretation often becomes immediately doubtful. Further error is then inevitable in scribal transmission, resulting either from carelessness in transcribing what was already only half intelligible or from attempts to improve the text of the exemplar. Textual difficulties are fortunately not vitally serious in the verse in the saga of Gisli, where all but two or three of the stanzas can be satisfactorily reconstituted. Even in the exceptions there is little or no confusion in the manuscript tradition over certain single words, which may have some weight in any argument about the date of origin of this poetry. The other basic difficulty results from the extremely conservative nature of verse composed in the scaldic tradition. In metre, language and style this verse remained fundamentally the same for more than two centuries. It would have been perfectly possible for a poet around the year 1200, well schooled in his native traditions, to compose a verse, particularly on some conventional subject like a battle, indistinguishable in any particular from a verse on a similar subject made around the year 1000. It is thus often impossible to decide whether a given verse is genuinely as old as a saga may report it to be, although in other cases, as in the saga of Gisli, a comparative study of the language and style of the verse may lead to a more positive conclusion.

There are three main hypotheses that may be held about the origin of verse such as that found in the saga of Gisli. It may be the work of Gisli in the tenth century, as it purports to be. It may be the work of the author of the saga we now have. It may also be the creation of a man who lived some time between Gisli's death and the time when the saga was written. In this case we should be obliged to presume that a story about Gisli's life and death accompanied the verse. The verse in the present text does not make a story on its own, and it could hardly have existed independently. All these opinions about the verse in the saga of Gisli have in fact been held by earlier critics. There have been various refinements. Some people have been bold enough to distinguish this or that verse as Gisli's and this or that verse as spurious. Others have considered that the poetry was Gisli's in origin, but that it has been 'reworked' in the twelfth century. Others again have detected different 'layers' in the verse, some old, some young, without necessarily attributing any of it to Gisli himself.

It must unfortunately be said that in such a relatively small corpus of verse we do not possess the means to make any confident distinction between genuine and spurious or between 'layers' of any kind. A single certain exception is the verse 'Not every dream avails me', which is in rhyme—a feature so rarely present in early Norse verse that the possibility that Gisli composed it may be dismissed out of hand. Yet it must be noted that this verse occurs as one of a sequence and shows marked similarity in ideas and phrasing to the stanzas it accompanies. Either it is an imitation, or all these verses must be regarded as one man's variations on a theme and allowed to stand or fall together. In fact so much of the verse shows common characteristics that at any rate the bulk of it must be considered the work of one man or, something which amounts to the same thing in this context, as the work of a closely related 'school' of poets. That the quality of the stanzas should vary—some are good, most mediocre—does not of course conflict with such conclusions.

We can thus do no more than test the three main hypotheses mentioned above. Consider first the possibility that the author of the saga wrote prose and verse together. It is usually considered right to dismiss such a possibility if there is disagreement between what the prose says and what the verse says. This is obviously not a rule that can be applied uncritically, for a man working within the exigencies of metrical form might well find himself forced to say more or less than he said in his prose, or even something rather different. (This is what tends to happen in a metrical translation of the verse, too.) But it must be allowed that when there are marked discrepancies between the two, or when there appears to be verbal or other evidence that the prose is based on the verse, then the probability becomes strong enough to warrant the conclusion that one man was not responsible for both. This seems to be the case with the saga of Gisli. The most striking example of discrepancy between prose and verse is found in the stanza 'Loud in my mind, lady', p. 55. In the last line in the Icelandic the verse has the word *læmingja*, and in the introductory prose the writer speaks of 'birds called *læmingar*'. Although no one perfectly understands what the word means in the verse, all are agreed that it cannot possibly mean any sort of bird, and a different interpretation offered in another manuscript of the saga is no more successful. (The unintelligible words have not been included in the translation.) The original author must have misunderstood the verse transmitted to him. A different sort of discrepancy may be seen in the last verse, 'Sheer goddess of shower', p. 58, which seems to imply that Gisli and his wife are at some distance from each other, which hardly squares with the prose. The writer here adds the remark: 'This is Gisli's last verse', and this also suggests that he had it from some source other than his own imagination. There are other occasions where verse and prose are less obviously connected and consistent than one might expect if both are to be ascribed to the same man (e.g. 'Fell I not nor failed at', p. 24; 'Word has come from northward', p. 32; 'Loud they tongue my lady', p. 50; 'Sorrow will you sever', p. 52). It is also important that the construction of the latter part of the saga, with its concentration on the last seven years of Gisli's outlawry, appears to depend on the dream-verse, 'Wife, land of the wave fire', p. 33, where the seven fires of the dream foretell the number of years he has yet to live.

If the verse cannot be by the author of the saga, we must decide between the other possibilities. The versification, the language and the ideas must be set against what we know of the poetry and beliefs of the tenth century on the one hand, and of later times on the other.

The versification can unfortunately tell us little, except in the case of the rhymed stanza mentioned earlier. There are certain irregularities in the internal rhymes of the stanzas, and these can be paralleled in some verse from the tenth century. In long poems from the twelfth century we find either an extremely correct traditional metrical form or else novel and experimental variations on the old forms, where licence has been turned into principle. In informal and occasional verse preserved from this period, however, we also find much irregularity. Metrically the verse in the story of Gisli might belong either to the early or to the late period.

Certain archaic forms in the language of the verse are equally inconclusive. The strength of the scaldic tradition ensured the long preservation of ancient forms, often metrically convenient, which had disappeared from the language of speech and written prose. A more positive result may be obtained, however, by considering words that appear in the kennings, the figurative expressions that are the chief feature of scaldic style. In most cases it is impossible to say that a word or phrase belongs to any distinctive period, but in the verse in the saga of Gisli there is a significant number of instances, some twenty to twenty-five spread throughout the stanzas, where the usage can in effect only be paralleled in poetry composed after about 1100. It might be argued that in such cases Gisli's verse was the source from which the other examples are derived. This argument might have some weight if there were any evidence outside the saga to show that Gisli was a poet, or if the poetry attributed to him were of such quality that it might have been justly influential. Neither of these conditions can be met. A more credible conclusion is that the poetry in the saga was composed in a twelfth-century *milieu*.

The material available for such comparison varies greatly in extent, and some uncertainty must always remain in such a study. Two or three examples, where the evidence is less disputable, may serve as illustration. In the original of the verse 'Sorrow, joy's dour slayer', p. 19, there is a kenning, *snáka tún*, 'field of snakes', which means gold. The word *snákr* occurs once in an anonymous verse assigned to the late tenth century. Its first use in a kenning is from the mid-eleventh century, in a humorous verse, where one feels that the word itself was probably part of the joke. All the other instances, six in the word's ordinary meaning, ten in kennings (chiefly for gold), are from the twelfth century and later. In the stanza 'Giant-bane Grim's grave mound', p. 26, there is a kenning, *lundr ábranda*, 'tree of river-brands', i.e. tree of gold, a man. (The second element may be read differently, but the interpretation remains the same.) It happens that the word *lundr* in kennings where a word or phrase for gold is the defining element occurs only once otherwise in an early stanza—attributed to a Norwegian in the early eleventh century—whereas all the other instances, at least a dozen, are found in verse from the twelfth century and later. In the stanza 'Wife, land of the wave fire',

p. 33, there is a kenning for gold, *Iðja galdr*, 'Idi's magic chant'. Of the seven other instances of this mythological name in such kennings, five occur in verse generally assigned to the twelfth century or later, and the other two are in stanzas which almost certainly belong to the same period. In the stanza 'Wife-veil-hearted wavering', p. 28, and again in the dream-verse 'Splendid sea-flame goddess', p. 48, the word *lægir*, 'sea', occurs in kennings with the form, 'fire of the sea', i.e. gold. The word is found once, not as part of a kenning, in a fragment of three lines of unknown authorship that has been assigned to the tenth century (all kinds of uncertainty attend such a dating). Otherwise there are five examples where it has its straightforward meaning and four examples where it is used in kennings for gold, all from the twelfth century or later.

The twelfth century was characterized earlier as an age of antiquarian interests. It was also an age when much poetry was composed. Poems in honour of great men continued to be fashionable and profitable; the occasion could still produce its lampoon, the love affair its lyric. There can be no doubt but that much new verse was composed then for the benefit of stories told about Icelanders of earlier ages, as embellishment, as a simple exercise in virtuosity, or as an integral part of the narrative. When such verse was remembered it was not in connection with a poet or story-teller of the twelfth century but in connection with the tenth-century hero in whose story it figured. Combined with authentic early verse, it was then available to saga-authors of the thirteenth century, who, on occasion, doubtless added new verses of their own to the canon.

The most important and novel compositions of the period, however, are a number of poems in scaldic metre and manner on religious subjects. In the century or so following the Conversion of the Icelanders (A.D. 1000) it appears that poets generally aimed at a simpler diction and avoided the use of kennings that had a marked heathen import—those containing the names or by-names of the heathen gods, for example, although they were certainly familiar with them. In other verse, and particularly in heroic verse in an eddaic style dealing with heroes of times long past, heathen references were still allowed. Such references might after all be part of the 'historicity' of the subject-matter, for few Christians in that early period doubted the existence, once effective, of the heathen divinities, and they had a sympathetic regard for their pagan forefathers as misguided rather than wicked in following the ancient faith. By the middle of the twelfth century, at any rate, the stigma of paganism in poetic diction was no longer strongly felt, and even the diction of these great religious poems shows itself to be much influenced by the vocabulary and kennings of pre-Christian poets. In 1154 the priest Einar Skulason composed a fine poem in honour of St Olaf. It is called *Geisli*, 'Sun-beam', and this theme of light is worked out in its many Christian connotations in the poem. Einar uses some expressions, however, which can only be understood by reference to heathen poetic usage and the heathen mythology that lay behind it. His mastery of the ancient poetic tradition is shown, moreover, in the diction and complex kennings of his fragmentarily preserved 'Axe-verses', on a purely secular and warlike theme. Another notable poem is the *Harmsól*, 'Grief-sun', by Gamli, a member of the Augustinian house of Þykkvibær in the south of Iceland. This is a confession of sin and plea for mercy and it makes a much more personal impact than *Geisli* does. The description of the second coming of the Lord to judge the world contains imagery reminiscent of the description of the doom of the gods in the *Völuspá*, the great poem from the close of the heathen period in Iceland. In another poem, the anonymous and mystical *Sólarljóð*, 'Song of the Sun', we have a series of visions seen by the soul at the moment of the creature's dissolution in death. The symbolism here is fully Christian in purport, but contains many echoes from pagan mythology. By the end of the heathen period in Iceland men's ideas about death and the fate of mankind and the world had already been influenced by Christian apocalyptic themes. Later, in the early Christian period, it was precisely in visions of death and judgment that Christian and pagan ideas and images could most easily coalesce.

This active twelfth-century return to the ancient pre-Christian poetry is in line with the antiquarian interests in the historical field that were mentioned earlier. There is a certain scholastic element in the correctness of metre displayed in a poem like *Geisli*, and from about the middle of the twelfth century we have the first poem which is also a metrical handbook—the poem *Háttalykill*, 'Key of metres', composed in part by the Orkney earl, Rognvald kali, where different stanzas illustrate different metrical and stylistic forms. Similarly, as we have seen, there is much imitation of early diction. The poets did not rest there, however. We have poems that show metrical experiment and we see how old kennings may appear in new variations, variations that would not, it seems, have been to the taste of an earlier age. The mythological references and names often have a learned flavour. It is not surprising to find that certain things in the verse of the saga of Gisli are most closely paralleled in poems on religious subjects from this period. The mythological name *Sjöfn*, for example, which is used in kennings in the stanzas 'If dreams true lines draw me', p. 36, and 'Band goddess bent to me', p. 55, is only found otherwise in the *Plácitúsdrápa*, a scaldic version of the legend of St Eustace and his family.

Some of the younger heroic poems of the *Edda* and much of the poetry in eddaic metres now preserved in the so-called 'legendary' sagas are also thought to be from the end of the eleventh or from the twelfth century. Much of this kind of verse is marked by a raw sentimentality, emotional exaggeration and a certain lack of dignity. A possible connection exists between one of these poems, the Second Lay of Gudrun, which in its present shape is best assigned to a date not earlier than about 1050, and the verse 'Giant-bane Grim's grave mound' in the story of Gisli. In the Icelandic this begins, *Teina sák í túni*, and the same word-pair is also found in the first lines of stanza 40 in the Gudrun poem: *Hugða ek hér í túni | teina fallna*. If the echo is not accidental then the verse in the saga must be the derivative. The poet's interest in the story of Gudrun is shown by his application of that story to Thordis's situation in the story of Gisli, made explicit in the verse 'Wife-veil-hearted wavering'.

It remains to consider the content of the dream-verses. People who consider the verse to be substantially authentic have naturally regarded the dream-verses as a credible expression of a man's inner conflict, torn between paganism and Christianity. This must have been precisely the effect the twelfth-century poet hoped to achieve. The idea was part of his reconstruction of Gisli's story, and it is repeated, but not much emphasized, in the remarks of the prose—that Gisli gave up sacrificing after his visit to Denmark and that the dream woman bids Gisli give up the old faith—although in the story the idea of black magic is also introduced as a cause of Gisli's disturbed state. Some of the diverse elements in the symbolism of the dream women and their relationship with Gisli can be disentangled. Like the language, they too point to a late date for the verse's composition.

In the first dream in which Gisli's good dream women appears he is introduced into a hall where seven fires burn; they foretell

119

the number of years he has yet to live, and the dream woman tells him how he must conduct himself. Gisli is greeted by the occupants of the hall whom, according to the prose, he recognizes as kinsfolk and friends. The latter idea is a well-preserved piece of ancient belief about the other world found in many sources, but the combination of prophecy and moral advice is a motive from Christian legend. Fredrik Paasche has further shown that the latter half of the stanza, 'Hold your blade from bloodshed', is closely based on words from the half-canonical 2 Esdras ii. 21: 'Heal the broken and the weak, laugh not a lame man to scorn, defend the maimed, and let the blind man come into the sight of my clearness'. In other stanzas describing Gisli's relations with the good dream woman he is invited to a splendid house, where he is to come after death, he is promised healing, wealth and command over the dream woman herself; in a stanza shortly before his death Gisli describes how a weeping dream woman binds up his wounds. It is difficult to see how far the poet intends us to understand some kind of erotic relationship between Gisli and the dream woman: they are to live together in the splendid house, he is to command her. There is nothing to support such ideas in what we know of the supernatural female figures of Icelandic folk-belief, who are discussed below. The poet is chiefly concerned to stress the comforts that Gisli is to enjoy, in contrast to his outlawed state on earth—certainly the idea of rest is uppermost in the singularly feeble description of the bed to which his dream woman leads him in the stanza 'Splendid sea-flame goddess'. There are overtones that can as well be attributed to Christian ideas of paradise, often conveyed in vague but still concrete terms. Life itself was an outlawed existence, cut off from heaven, our true home. There are phrases in that same book of Esdras which strike the same note as the poet of Gisli's verses: there are laid up for us dwellings of health and safety; a paradise wherein are security and medicine, where plenteousness is made ready and rest is allowed. In the *Harmsól* paradise is a place of delight and prosperity, a place where there is abundance of pleasure. It is altogether a better place, and the poet's words, 'Years are few . . . until a better time,' in the stanza 'Bend your eyes, band goddess', echoes this common Christian idea of the next world, found in *Geisli* ('a better light'), in *Leiðarvísan*, a twelfth-century poem in praise of Sunday (paradise is a 'nobler, more desirable and better place than all'), and in a poem in honour of Bishop Pall Jonsson, who died in 1211 (he 'prepared himself for a better [place]').

The idea of a supernatural woman inviting a hero home through death is found elsewhere in early Norse verse, and it was probably no more than a literary motive to the poet of the verses in the saga of Gisli. It occurs in the ancient pagan poem, *Ynglingatal*, from *c*. 900, and differently, half a century later, in *Hákonarmál*, where the valkyries, 'choosers of the slain', appear in full panoply to summon King Hakon and a great host to Valhall, the home of the gods. Then it occurs in a stanza attributed to a man called Bjorn Hitdœlakappi, supposed to have been composed in 1024, where the messenger is the 'helmeted valkyrie of God'. A similar idea is found in the eleventh- or twelfth-century eddaic poem, the *Atlamál*, and there are echoes of it in *Sólarljóð* and in the *Krákumál*, an antiquarian and romantic viking poem from the twelfth century. The idea of death as an invitation home figures more than once in the religious poems of this period, although the supernatural woman does not appear in them.

The supernatural women of Gisli's dreams have complex origins. Three kinds of pagan conception that were given embodiment in female form seem to have contributed to them. First, in early times men believed in the existence of a *fylgja*, or 'fetch', a tutelary spirit attached to a family or an individual; the *fylgja* was often thought to manifest itself in female form. Second, they believed in the minor divinities called valkyries, 'choosers of the slain', goddesses of battle and thus associated with carnage and death. Third, they knew of divinities called *dísir*, minor unnamed goddesses who represented powers of fertility; they were celebrated in private acts of cult-worship, especially in the sacrificial feasts held at the beginning of winter (cf. p. 73), and they were connected with the major god and goddess, Frey and Freyja, who had voluptuousness as their chief characteristic and the promotion of fertility as their chief function. These varied female figures do not seem to have been kept entirely distinct from one another. The *dísir*, at any rate, celebrated in the cult-acts of a private circle of family and friends, seem to have been regarded as attached to that circle, and thus not very different from the family *fylgja*. It is clear that Gisli's good dream woman has something of the nature of the *fylgja*, and his bad dream woman has something of the nature of the valkyrie. The attitude of the bad dream woman towards Gisli and her influence on his fate can be interpreted in the light of ancient ideas about the *dísir*, although in this poetry they have been decisively modified by Christian ideas.

121

It has been common enough to consider divine retribution the cause of personal and public disaster. In earlier times it was usually as much what a man failed to do as what he did that was believed to call forth divine anger. If a man stopped paying the customary sacrifices to the *dísir*, for example, and suffered afterwards, it was not to be wondered at, for the *dísir* were angry. This idea, that the *dísir* might turn from friends into dangerous enemies, was undoubtedly alive in pagan Iceland, and it would be particularly alive at the time when the cult was threatened with neglect on a large scale. In the period just before the Conversion there was evidently much discussion of the religious question and zealous pagans became hard and reactionary. They were not only attached by strong ties of tradition and custom to the old faith, but must also have been full of horror at the consequences of its abandonment. That the anger of the *dísir* was resorted to in order to explain an otherwise inexplicable disaster is shown by the story of Thidrandi. He was a son of a prominent chieftain, who favoured Christianity, and he died about the time when his father accepted the new faith. The story told of his death is that at a feast at the time of the Winter Nights—it is to be presumed that the usual sacrifices were not being made—he went outside by night, and he was attacked and mortally wounded by nine women, clothed in black. The story calls them the *fylgjur* of the family, but also refers to them as *dísir*, who thus took their own last vengeful sacrifice from Thidrandi's race. While he was attacked he is supposed to have seen nine women, clad in white and riding white horses—these are called the 'better *dísir*', who on this occasion could be of no avail, but represented the better faith that was to come.

Some reminiscence of the angry *dís* or *fylgja* may also appear in Gisli's bad dream woman. She comes to torment him because he adheres to the good dream woman, and, like the author of the prose, the poet of the verses doubtless reckoned that Gisli had given up sacrificing. The idea is an analogue of that in the story of Thidrandi. What cannot possibly have pagan origin in these tales is, of course, the duality, the hostility between separately personified spirits, representing pagan and Christian, bad and good. Here we move into a Christian world with its ideas of good and bad angels attendant on the individual and its many stories of visions in which angels and devils contend for the possession of the soul (the devils often 'carry on hideously', in much the same way as Gisli's dream woman). Such stories and ideas were

122

undoubtedly known in Iceland, and some examples of them are found in translations amongst early Icelandic religious literature.

The supernatural women of pagan belief seem to have lived on as the natural divine emissaries of early Icelandic Christendom. Bjorn Hitdœlakappi's verse with its picture of the 'helmeted valkyrie of God' was mentioned earlier. At one point in the *Sólarljóð* the man is bidden to 'pray that the *dísir*, confidantes of the Lord, may be favourable to you in their thoughts'! Three women appear in a dream-vision vouchsafed in the course of one of St Olaf's miracles, first recorded in the *Passio et miracula beati Olavi*, written *c.* 1170 by the Norwegian archbishop Eystein Erlendsson. In the so-called *Dream of Thorstein Sidu-Hallsson* (Thorstein was a brother of Thidrandi), his death is foretold in three verses pronounced to him by three dream women. The verses are obscure, but the Norns, a valkyrie and God jostle strangely in them.

We see at any rate some of the diverse strands that mingle in Gisli's dream women. They are fluid and inconsistent in themselves—in the stanza 'Sorrow will you sever', p. 52, for example, the bad dream woman (if the author of the prose has sorted it out properly) is undoubtedly an angelic figure sent from another world, but in the following stanzas she is the angry *dís*, the valkyrie who washes Gisli in blood. The elements of which they are compounded, motives from poetry and story-telling, pagan reminiscences and Christian doctrine, show that they are no more than the poet's imaginings and that they have no first-hand connection with any kind of authentic folk-belief. Even if there were no other evidence, the content of the verses in the saga of Gisli would show that they must be the product of a Christian age.

5

IF THE VERSE in the saga is to be attributed to the latter part of the twelfth century, or to the period about 1200, and is not the work of the author of the text we have, we must conclude that it was at the same time accompanied by a story told of Gisli's life and death. An answer to the question, What was that story like? can only be speculative. Judging by the verses which are part of the 'continuity' of the saga, it cannot have been very different in outline from the story we now have. Gisli and Vestein were friends and had been together at Sigrhadd's; Vestein was killed and Aud was sorrowful; Gisli killed Thorgrim, betrayed himself and was outlawed; he stayed some time with Ingjald; Thorkell was killed; at some stage Gisli is told that his wife thinks to betray him; finally Gisli himself fell in battle. The feeble verses, 'They would not at Thorsness', might provide information about the failure of the sons of Bjartmar to help Gisli as they should have done. Other verses in the saga either do not infer their own precise occasion or are not 'action-verses' at all, although the dream women must evidently have played an essential part in the earlier narrative. There is a good deal in the saga which is not covered by this outline, and it is possible to conceive the earlier narrative as providing a barer and at times different frame for the verses. The learning and historical imagination apparent in the poetry may easily be credited to the twelfth-century Icelander, probably a man in orders, in whose mind the story grew. One may perhaps wonder what part 'audience-participation' might play in the formation of such a story: some of the verses that embroider a single theme might have been contributed in this way. In the saga of Thorgils and Haflidi, for example—a text written soon after 1200 describing events that took place about 1120—there are three episodes where verses, showing verbal similarity, appear to be contributed by different men on the same subject. The process of composition must have gone on in Gisli's own locality, the West Fjords, where the verse would be firmly transmitted. We know nothing of the words of the story that was told with the poetry: they would not be learnt by rote by the few men who might learn the verse. Then at some time a man who knew the verse and had his own ideas about the events, the characters and the way in which they were to be presented, wrote the story of Gisli that we now have—the only form of the story to which the name 'saga' can be properly applied.

The saga of Gisli may waken interest and appreciation simply as a piece of story-telling. It gains in significance, however, and our understanding and appreciation of it are deepened, if we can relate it to the society in which it was created. It thus becomes important to decide when the saga was written.

The sagas of Icelanders are anonymous works, mostly preserved in manuscripts that are much younger than their original date of composition. Dating a saga involves the use of many skills—technical study of manuscripts, palaeography and language, on the one hand, and the study of historical background and literary form and relationships on the other. The first kind of approach may give direct and valuable evidence of the period of composition, but more often provides a *terminus ante quem* which, although reliable, is still so remote from the date of origin as to be of relatively small importance to the literary historian. In the case of the saga of Gisli, for example, such technical study would hardly enable us to say more than that it was written at some time in the thirteenth century. As for the study of historical background, it does occasionally appear as if some Icelandic event of the thirteenth century has provided a motive that has been made use of in saga literature, and later on it will be suggested that the saga of Gisli may have some such connections with real life. More often, however, we need to arrive at a date for a saga's composition before the contemporary scene can be considered with any profit. This, as will be seen later, is also true of the saga of Gisli, whose genesis and peculiar features receive some illumination when the work is set against a certain background at a certain time.

When no direct evidence is available, a saga may be dated most reliably by a demonstration of its literary relationships. There are enough fixed points in the history of early Icelandic literature to give a reasonable hope of relating a given saga to one or more of them. Of particular importance in this respect is the *Book of the Settlements* (see p. 100 above), which was used as an authoritative source by many saga-writers. Consideration of the differences and similarities between the information contained in its various recensions and that given in a saga may throw light on both the manner and the time of the saga's composition.

The settlement of Thorbjorn is noted in the *Book of the Settlements*, and all the other principal characters of the saga of Gisli occur in its genealogies (a translation of the part dealing with settlement in Arnarfjord and Dyrafjord is given on pp. 86–8). There are few details given in the *Book*, but it is surprising how many discrepancies there are between its account and that given in the saga. The chief of these are as follows: Vestein Vegeirsson, according to the *Book*, was the settler in Haukadal and he gave half the valley to Thorbjorn; in the saga Vestein is a Norwegian who lodges with Bjartmar, and Thorbjorn buys land in Haukadal from some man unnamed. In the *Book* the wife of Thorkell, Gisli's brother, is said to have been Sigrid Slettu-Bjorn's daughter;

in the saga she is said to have been Asgerd Thorbjorn's daughter. (Neither of these women is known in any other source; we have no idea who Asgerd's father is supposed to be, either, but Sigrid's father was a well-known settler.) According to the *Book*, Ingjald in Hergilsey was the son of the settler who gave his name to the island, while the saga says that he was related to Gisli and a tenant of Bork the stout. There are some other discrepancies in the matter of Vestein's family (cf. the passages from the *Book* given on pp. 86–8), but enough has been said to show that the author of the saga of Gisli did not know the *Book of the Settlements*.

This matter in the *Book of the Settlements* can be traced back as far as a recension made some time before 1245, and it probably depends on twelfth-century sources. A later recension of the *Book*, made in the third quarter of the thirteenth century, shows influence from the saga, in the mention of Ari, son of whey-Thorbjorn, for example, although the major differences noted above are not disturbed. This version does say, however, that Ingjald helped Gisli and that, because of this, Bork exacted his islands from him. This can hardly be based on the saga we have, unless it has been used in combination with another source since lost. It will be seen that what material there is in the *Book* is meagre in the extreme. We might conclude either that little was known about the killing of Vestein and Thorgrim and Gisli's outlawry, or that it was such common knowledge that it required no special mention. The casual reference to Ingjald's help for Gisli in the younger recension of the *Book* would suggest the latter explanation, but we cannot base much on a source that is demonstrably younger than the saga. There is, however, another weighty reason for regarding it as the more probable.

This reason springs from our knowledge of the good conditions that existed for the survival of trustworthy information about these things in the family of Thordis, Gisli's sister. Thordis's son by Thorgrim was Snorri the Chieftain, one of the most influential men in Iceland about the time of the Conversion and on until his death in 1031. Snorri's daughter Thurid was born in 1024 and died in 1112 or 1113. She was one of the few people Ari the Learned (see p. 100) relied on for information about the past—he describes her as 'wise in many things and reliable in her learning'. We should also note that Eyjolf, Gisli's slayer, was Ari's great-great-grandfather. It is true that one may have doubts as to the way in which the events would be remembered in families whose forefathers had suffered much at Gisli's hands and who had finally avenged their injuries by bringing about his death. Certainly the saga as it is conceived and presented is unthinkable as part of the same *milieu* as that of Ari and his family, or even of the Sturlungs and Asbirnings, the most important of the thirteenth-century branches of Snorri the Chieftain's kin. Under the circumstances it is most likely that the information in the *Book of the Settlements*, such as it is, and the recording of the date of whey-Thorbjorn's arrival in Iceland in the annals (see note, p. 64), come from this background, while the saga springs from another.

That the central facts of the case were remembered with precision in Thordis's family is shown by the *Ævi Snorra goða* (*Life of Snorri the Chieftain*), which was mentioned earlier as an example of twelfth-century antiquarian interests (it is given in translation on p. 88). It is a record which has been plausibly linked with the name of Ari the Learned himself. There it says:

'Snorri the Chieftain was fourteen years old when he went abroad; he was abroad one winter. The winter following his return he lived at Helgafell with Bork the stout, his father's brother, and Thordis, his mother. This same autumn Eyjolf the grey, son of Thord bellower, killed Gisli, son of whey-Thorbjorn, and in the following spring, when Snorri was sixteen years old, he began to farm Helgafell, and he lived there for twenty years before Christianity was made law in Iceland and another eight years after that.'

This note about Snorri the Chieftain was amongst the sources used by the author of the *Eyrbyggja saga*, much of whose narrative is concerned with Snorri and his family. This saga was probably written about 1250, although it has also been reckoned to be from as early as 1220. The saga and the *Life* agree on the important chronological points mentioned in the passage quoted above. We may from them infer that Gisli's outlawry lasted at least fourteen, and possibly fifteen, years, since Snorri was born after his father's death and it may be reasonably assumed that Gisli was outlawed in the year following. The present version of the saga of Gisli does not agree with this precisely, although its chronology is somewhat vague in that, while it accounts for the first six years and the last seven of his outlawry, it does not make it clear whether we are to reckon on any interval between the two sections. In the other two versions of the saga of Gisli he is said to have been an outlaw for seventeen (or eighteen) years, a figure which may possibly be more original. But in either case it seems unlikely that the author of the saga of Gisli knew the *Life* or the *Eyrbyggja saga*. If the author had known the latter saga, moreover, he could not have made his error over the lifetime of Thorstein cod-biter (see note, p. 68), nor could he have ignored the authoritative statement in the *Eyrbyggja saga* that Thorgrim was killed when he was twenty-five—a fact which clearly makes the story of the death of Thorgrim's son at the hands of the Norwegians, told in chapter 7, an impossibility.

There is on the other hand no doubt but that the author of the *Eyrbyggja saga* made use of the saga of Gisli. In chapter 12 of that work we are told the bare facts: Thorgrim married Thordis and moved west to live, he killed Vestein at an autumn feast in Haukadal, and he was killed by Gisli at a feast at Saebol the following autumn. This bare record might depend on family tradition rather than on use of the saga of Gisli. In chapter 13, however, there is an account of Eyjolf's arrival at Bork's home to report the slaying of Gisli, and this account can only depend on the account in chapter 37 of the saga of Gisli. Such differences as exist between the two texts in these passages may be readily explained as due to the particular interests of the author of the *Eyrbyggja saga* and to his use of other sources—neither is it necessary to believe that he had the saga of Gisli open in front of him as he wrote. Antipathy to Bork is found in both the sagas, but this is not surprising—neither an admirer of Gisli nor an admirer of Snorri the Chieftain would have much to say in his favour.

The date of the *Eyrbyggja saga* gives a certain limit for the composition of the saga of Gisli. There is one other saga which is specifically related to the story of Gisli, the *Droplaugarsona saga*, in chapter 13 of which the death of a man called Helgi is described. He is stabbed in his bed and the episode is so like the death of Thorgrim in the saga of Gisli that a literary connection must exist between them. It is now generally agreed that the author of the saga of Gisli has borrowed from the *Droplaugarsona saga*, not least because the latter makes sense of such details in the story as the tying together of the cows' tails and the dressing of the slayer in underclothes, while the same things in the saga of Gisli remain pointless. There are also some minor similarities elsewhere between the two texts which, given the major loan just mentioned, are best explained as due to the influence of the *Droplaugarsona saga* on the saga of Gisli. A curious feature in this case of literary influence is that the two sagas could hardly have been written in places farther apart—*Droplaugarsona saga* in the far east of Iceland, the saga of Gisli in the far west. It is unfortunately impossible to date the *Droplaugarsona saga* with any precision, and the latest editor will do no more than assign it to the first forty years of the thirteenth century.

These demonstrable literary relationships thus provide a series, *Droplaugarsona saga*, the saga of Gisli, *Eyrbyggja saga*, in roughly the first half of the thirteenth century. This much is certain. On the basis of our knowledge of events in Iceland in the same period we may narrow the chronological field still further, although for the most part we are dealing with interesting speculation rather than certifiable fact.

In June 1221 a member of an important family in the south of Iceland was killed in a feud. The weapon used was a spear, 'which they called Greyflank and which they said Gisli whey-Thorbjorn's son had owned'. The spear's name is also given in an anonymous satirical verse on this killing. A spear with the same name, and doubtless the same weapon, was used again in a battle in 1238; this time it is described as 'an ancient spear with a damascened blade, not a very sturdy weapon' (it kept getting bent with use), but there is no reference to Gisli's ownership.

It is clear that something was known of Gisli and Greyflank by 1221. That knowledge was not necessarily connected with the saga we know and it might stem from independent tradition. People have always been fascinated by the instruments of notorious deeds, and several weapons in thirteenth-century Iceland have names suggestive of an illustrious blood-stained past. It is worth noting, however, that in the record referring to 1221 the writer seems careful, by his choice of phrase, not to underwrite the authenticity of the name of the spear or the attribution of ownership to Gisli: 'which *they called* Greyflank and which *they said* Gisli had owned'. This suggests that the writer, or his ultimate source-man, rather regarded the name and attribution as an unsubstantiated novelty. We are in no position to dispute the justice of such doubts. But if an ancient weapon had in fact been newly dubbed Gisli's Greyflank, it would not be unreasonable to assume that it was because a story of Gisli was then enjoying some vogue. It might be thought difficult, however, to conclude that that story was in all respects the same as the saga we know, for our present text gives small grounds for an assertion that Gisli owned Greyflank.

Now it is noteworthy that Greyflank does not figure in any

verse in the saga, and the story of its existence as a sword and its reforging as a spear is clearly invention (cf. note, p. 65). When it is remade it is described as having a damascened blade. The Greyflank used in the 1238 battle is also described as damascened —it is indeed the only spear described as such in all our numerous and various sources concerning Iceland in the twelfth and thirteenth centuries. It seems most likely that the description in the saga depends on a knowledge of this real contemporary spear. This weapon was evidently held in some superstitious regard. It is otherwise hard to see why this not very efficient blade was used in 1238. One reason for it is doubtless to be sought in the fact that the leader who bore it then in battle had as his chief enemy the half-brother of the man the spear had slain in 1221. But the ancient damascening may also have had its influence: as it is clearly believed to have had in the saga of Gisli.

The general conclusion from this consideration of the slight evidence available would be that by 1221, though not necessarily much earlier, some story of Gisli and Greyflank was current. With this story it would be natural to associate the verses which, as we have seen, must have been in existence before the present saga was written. In his literary treatment of the story the author of the saga we possess was moved, among other things, to write the prehistory of a real weapon known in his day and associated with Gisli. As far as can be seen, he is not likely to have done this until after the spear achieved notoriety in 1221.

Tentative confirmation of this conclusion may be drawn from a consideration of the saga of Gisli in relation to the career of a man called Aron Hjorleifsson. Aron was the most famous outlaw of his time, sentenced in 1222, as an act of personal and political vengeance. He maintained himself in Iceland for three years and then escaped to Norway. Several attempts were made to assassinate him while he was still in Iceland, but he was protected for some time by his kinsmen, the sons of Hrafn Sveinbjarnarson (see below), at Eyr on the north side of Arnarfjord. When things got too hot for them he was for long periods with a small farmer at a place called Geirthjofsfjord's Eyr. This is the place now called Krosseyri, on the north side of Geirthjofsfjord, only four miles from Gisli's own hiding-place and Aud's steading. There are one or two things in his career as an outlaw that are strikingly reminiscent of the saga of Gisli. While he is in Geirthjofsfjord, Aron repairs the boat of the farmer he lives with—Gisli is a handy man and makes boats for Ingjald in Hergilsey. In one of his moves

Aron takes a boat from Bardastrand and sails south across Breidafjord in it, after which he pushes it out to drift and it is later washed ashore—Gisli accepts a boat from his brother on Bardastrand, sails south to Hergilsey, and then pushes it out to drift; it is washed up and people believe he has been drowned. Aron had warning dreams too, but of course he and Gisli are by no means the only Icelanders who have experienced these. It is not unthinkable that Aron's concealment as an outlaw in the remote Geirthjofsfjord was in itself a factor which helped to renew and strengthen the local interest in the story of Gisli, from which arose the composition of the present saga. Gisli is not a literary portrait of Aron, any more than Thordis is modelled on the Jorunn we meet in *Hrafns saga* (see below), but there are one or two features in his saga which we may regard as borrowed from Aron's career, or which, at any rate, have been given a sharper edge in the narrative as a result of Aron's experiences.

The connections of the present saga of Gisli with the career of Aron Hjorleifsson would suggest a date of composition after, probably soon after, 1225, the year which saw Aron's departure for Norway. This fits in tidily enough with the place assigned to the saga of Gisli, between the *Droplaugarsona saga* and the *Eyrbyggja saga*.

6

THERE CAN BE little more than one generation separating the composition of the verses and the composition of the saga of Gisli that we know. Poet and author belonged to one *milieu*. It is of some interest to look at the one source which brings us into close touch with life in the West Fjords in the period around 1200. This is the saga of Hrafn Sveinbjarnarson. Hrafn was a direct descendant in the male line of the settler Geirthjof who took much land in Arnarfjord and first lived in Geirthjofsfjord. Hrafn's home was at Eyr, where his kinsman Aron Hjorleifsson was later protected by his sons, and this farm lies about half way, as the crow flies, between Geirthjofsfjord and Haukadal. Hrafn was killed in 1213 and his life was written about 1230 by a man who had been a member of his household circle.

The biography of Hrafn is undoubtedly tendentious, but we

get from it a remarkable impression of everyday reality, a world where men's minds were filled with a superstition that curiously blended the Christian and the pagan and a world where much verse was made. Hrafn himself was a distinguished chieftain and a famous physician, a devout man who had made pilgrimages to Rome, Saint-Gilles, Compostella and Canterbury, and a close friend of the fanatical Bishop Gudmund Arason. Through his wife and his sisters he had marriage connections with important families in the south and south-east and in the north of Iceland, the sort of connection that may be borne in mind when reflecting on the influence of the *Droplaugarsona saga*, written in the east of the country, on the saga of Gisli (cf. p. 128). On the evening before his death Hrafn had an Icelandic poem in honour of St Andrew recited to him, and after each verse he commented on its significance. Of the thirty-three stanzas in various metres quoted in his saga, eleven are from a long poem composed about Hrafn after his death, while the remainder are occasional verses contributed by half a dozen different people. Three of the poets belonged to Hrafn's own household, and of these one was his close kinsman and another was a monk. Four of the verses are ominous 'dream-verses'. The most striking of these is one of the many dreams and portents experienced in Hrafn's district just before he was attacked and killed by the man, Thorvald Snorrason, who, for reasons that are not entirely clear, had become his bitter enemy. A certain man dreamt that he saw the sky full of moons, as many as the stars, some full and some half, some bigger and some smaller, waxing and waning. Then he saw a man beside him, who spoke this verse:

> '*See where the souls*
> *Of sinful men*
> *Are whirled away*
> *The worlds between.*
> *Spirits suffer*
> *In the serpent's jaws,*
> *Strong sun shivers—*
> *Should you not waken?*'

This is most strongly reminiscent of the *Song of the Sun*, the *Sólarljóð*, the twelfth-century visionary poem that was spoken of earlier. Altogether it may be said that the poet of the verses in the saga of Gisli would fit naturally into the intellectual and poetic background portrayed in the saga of Hrafn.

It is one of the compelling features of the co-called 'contemporary' sagas, those like the saga of Hrafn that describe twelfth- and thirteenth-century events on the basis of first-hand sources, that they bring us into such close touch with reality that we are, as it were, scraped on a raw nerve. The writers of these works described people and events they knew personally; some things doubtless had to be suppressed, but other less relevant matter might often be included if the writer was interested in it. And what some of these authors see fit to report does not entirely square with what the authors of the sagas of Icelanders for the most part found suitable, realistic though the latter are. In this respect the author of the saga of Gisli, preoccupied as he is with the bonds of emotion between brother and sister, husband and wife, displays an interest more akin to the authors of some of the contemporary sagas. The author of the saga of Hrafn is a man of similar kind. In matters that have little or no relevance to the progress of the action, he is willing to dwell on people's emotions, by which he himself was clearly affected. At one point, for instance, he notes the long periods of dejection suffered by a man who grieves for his dead wife. On another occasion he notes the sorry plight of a household where everyone had been tied up to prevent any message of an impending attack being carried to Hrafn, where the children cried and their mothers and fathers were unable to help them. He also records the remarkable career of a woman called Jorunn, sister of Thorvald Snorrason, Hrafn's enemy. She begins by having an affair with her brother-in-law, Svein, and this prompts her half-brother, Thord, to arrange an attack on Svein's life—he is only wounded, but the attacker and another man are killed. She is then abducted, willingly it seems, by a priest called Magnus. These two successfully elude the pursuit of another of Jorunn's former lovers, and finally, with Jorunn disguised as a man in the best romantic tradition, they escape abroad to Norway. There marriage and many children are the prosaic end. Jorunn and the Thordis we know in the saga of Gisli have something in common.

The strange and fundamental differences between the saga of Gisli and the other sagas of Icelanders appear less remarkable when it is seen against the real background of the West Fjords in the early years of the thirteenth century. We must be grateful to the author for his moving study of human character and his masterly narrative of suspense and action. And our interest and appreciation can only be deepened by the story's revelation, franker than in any other of the sagas of Icelanders, of the mind of the author and the character of the age and locality in which he lived.

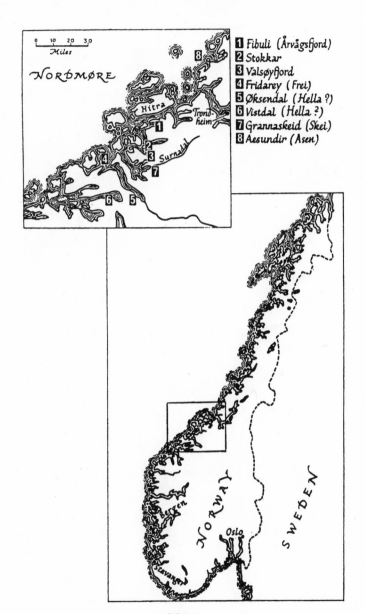

1 Fibuli (Årvågsfjord)
2 Stokkar
3 Valsøyfjord
4 Fridarey (Frei)
5 Øksendal (Hella?)
6 Vistdal (Hella?)
7 Grannaskeid (Skei)
8 Aesundir (Asen)

Map 1

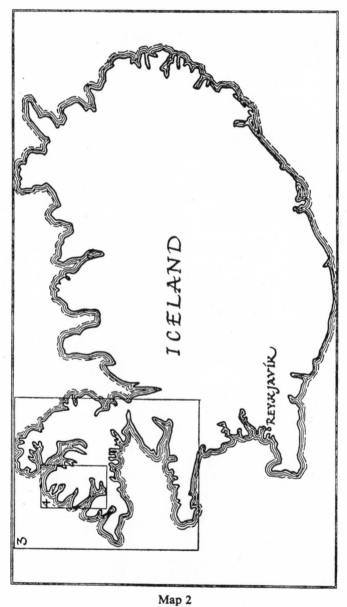

Map 2
The rectangles numbered 3 and 4 indicate the area covered by
Maps 3 and 4

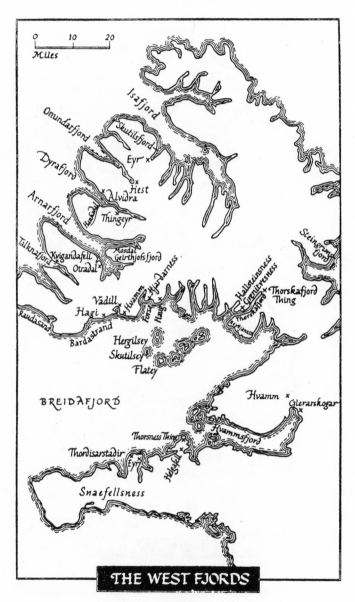

THE WEST FJORDS

Map 3

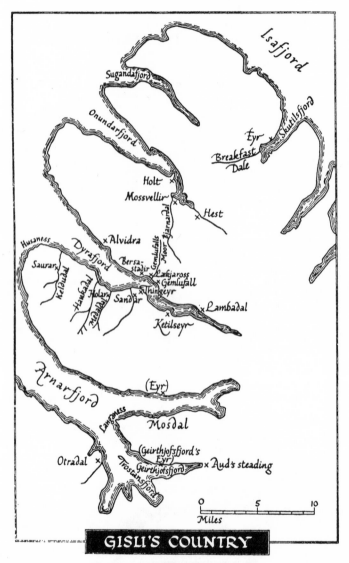

GISLI'S COUNTRY

Map 4

Eyr, the home of Hrafn Sveinbjarnarson, and Geirthjofsfjord's
Eyr, the hiding-place of Aron Hjorleifsson (see the Essay,
pp. 130–1) are also included.

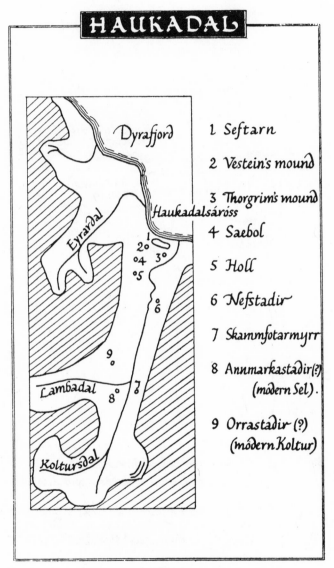

HAUKADAL

1 Seftarn

2 Vestein's mound

3 Thorgrim's mound

4 Saebol

5 Holl

6 Nefstadir

7 Skammfotarmyrr

8 Annmarkastadir(?)
  (modern Sel).

9 Orrastadir (?)
  (modern Koltur)

Dyrafjord

Haukadalsáróss

Eyrardal

Lambadal

Koltursdal

Plan 1

In the translation Skammfotarmyrr is called Shortleg's marshland and Orrastadir Heathcock's steading.

HAUKADAL

Dyrafjord

Haukadalsáróss
(Mouth of the Haukadal River)

This end of
the pond
was marsh
and reed
grown.

THE RUSH POND

Games played
here on ice

Vestein's
mound

Thorgrims
mound

N

Saebol

The Brook

Holl

.... Paths to brook from Holl and Saebol
----- Probable line of Vestein's approach to Holl

Approximate distances: the rush pond - 400
yards long.
from Saebol to Holl - 250 yards.

Plan 2

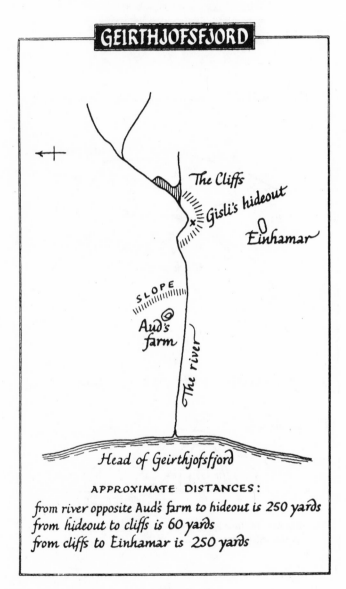

GEIRTHJOFSFJORD

The Cliffs

Gisli's hideout

Einhamar

SLOPE

Aud's farm

The river

Head of Geirthjofsfjord

APPROXIMATE DISTANCES:

from river opposite Aud's farm to hideout is 250 yards
from hideout to cliffs is 60 yards
from cliffs to Einhamar is 250 yards

Plan 3

GEIRTHJOFSFJORD

THE CLIFFS *seen from the hide-out c. 60 yards away*

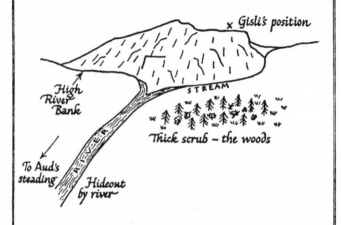

x Gisli's position

High
River
Bank

STREAM

RIVER

To Aud's
steading

Hideout
by river

Thick scrub – the woods

EINHAMAR *seen from c. 100 yards away*

Gisli stood here
on the ledge

Height c. 24 feet

Base length c. 120 feet

It is easy to climb up
to the ledge here.

(*Opposite*)

EINHAMAR

Across the river to the south-east of the farmstead in Geirthjofs-fjord the mountain slope rises steadily, in the space of half a mile, to about 650 feet above sea level. Up to the 400-foot line the slope is covered by thick birch scrub, the trees often 10–12 feet in height. At about 650 feet there is a shelf that rises more gently—some 60 feet in 200 yards—and after that the slope mounts steadily until it reaches some 2,000 feet at about one and a half miles from the sea. At the 650-foot line and above it there are many precipitous rock walls.

Einhamar is a small outcrop set amongst the scrub at about 250 feet above sea level. It stands out as a low grey bluff. The diagram makes it look isolated, but it must be remembered that the slope continues to rise above and around it and that the flat top of Einhamar is no more than a small projecting shelf in that slope. Thus, although the rock face of the bluff can only be easily climbed at the place indicated, a couple of minutes' scramble up the hillside at either end of the bluff will bring one to the top. One is then standing on the flat surface of the outcrop a few feet above the farther projecting ledge where Gisli made his defence.

The preceding maps and plans are based upon the work of Sigurður Vigfússon in *Árbók hins íslenzka Fornleifafélags*, 1883, 1–70; Magnus Olsen, *Norrøne studier* (1938), 272–88 (also in *Aarbøger for nordisk Oldkyndighed*, 1918, 41–60); and Anne Holtsmark, *Studies in the Gísla saga* (Studia Norvegica 6; 1951), especially pp. 28–32.

Index

These abbreviations are used: d. = daughter; s. = son; w. = wife; D. = in Denmark; N. = in Norway.

144